# THE
# CREATIVE
# STENCIL
## Source Book

# THE
# CREATIVE
# STENCIL
## Source Book
### 200 inspiring and original motifs

## PATRICIA MEEHAN
### *with* Les Meehan

COLLINS & BROWN

First published in Great Britain in 1998 by
Collins & Brown Limited
London House, Great Eastern Wharf
Parkgate Road, London SW11 4NQ

British Library Cataloguing-in-Publication Data:
A catalogue record for this title is available from the British Library.

3 5 7 9 8 6 4 2

ISBN 1 85585 609 3 (hardback edition)
ISBN 1 85585 658 1 (paperback edition)

Conceived, edited and designed by
Collins & Brown Limited

Editorial Director: Sarah Hoggett
Editor: Corinne Asghar
Designer: Helen Collins
Digital artwork: Alison Lee, Simon Ward-Hastelow

Reproduction by Grafiscan, Italy
Printed and bound in China

# CONTENTS

# INTRODUCTION

Welcome one and all. I cannot believe that it is eight years since I wrote the first of 'The Stencil Source Books'.

I find it gratifying that more and more people are turning to stencilling to decorate their homes, their clothes and special gifts for friends. Only a week ago I was browsing through an art supply shop when a lady tapped me on the shoulder. She asked me if I knew anything about stencilling as she was in a quandary as to which paints to buy. She went on to say that she was a schoolteacher and wanted to show her pupils how to decorate T-shirts. Needless to say she left the shop with the correct paints and brushes and with lots of useful advice. I hope that she has gone on to inspire the next generation of stencillers.

Stencilling is a creative activity. We make our designs, choose our colour schemes and decorate our homes with our own artistic flair.

It is well within your capabilities to produce a beautiful stencilled motif. Then, once you have taken that first step you can turn your hand to stencilling anything. I have always said that once you have successfully stencilled your first petal you can go on to stencil the whole garden. The techniques are the same no matter how complex your design. No doubt you will find that you will want to go on and stencil more and more complex designs using lots of different colours, shapes and surfaces.

In this book I have made lots of new designs and again used them in the projects that you can see in the photographs. There are also some new techniques on these pages, including three-dimensional stencilling, which is quite new in England and very inspiring. Some of the projects are simple, some of them are more complicated. I hope that, in this way, the book caters for the beginner and the experienced stenciller alike. There are traditional designs and some more unusual subjects for you to try.

I hope that you will enjoy reading the text as well as taking inspiration from the photographs and designs. There are lots of ideas in these chapters that you can either use or adapt to your own requirements.

Brushes, paints and stencils have all become much more readily available since I first began stencilling with my two brushes and two pots of paint. The choices now before you are vast and the colouring effects that you can achieve are impossible to number. It is all so exciting. For the new stenciller it can also be quite daunting. My advice is to just take your time and look around until you find exactly what you want. Trace out the designs that you would like to use from the book. You can photocopy them up or down in size then colour them in to find the colour scheme that pleases you.

It would be lovely to hear from some of you to find out how you have used the stencil designs from the previous books or this, the newest 'Stencil Source Book'. I know that people buy the books but it is so rewarding to know that people have used them to take designs and ideas from and not just to prop up a wobbly table.

I hope that my enthusiasm for stencilling has inspired you and helped you to enjoy your stencilling. Once you have released your creativity you will have the freedom to use colour and design anywhere in your home.

# EGYPTIAN DREAM

*Oases in the rolling sands, camel trains along the Nile, bazaars and hieroglyphs, the mystery of Sphinx and the majesty of the Pyramids: the designs of ancient Egypt will inspire you to create your own stencilled treasures.*

*PREVIOUS PAGE*
*A layer of blue paint, then cream, was distressed to age the surface of the box before stencilling. The colour scheme is based on wall paintings from Egyptian tombs.*

*ABOVE*
*The green of the oasis was over-painted with a blue glaze then stencilled at ceiling and skirting levels with a border of green palm leaves entwined with blue ribbon. Small groupings of reeds in gold and green are dotted around the walls.*

Egypt is a wonderfully vibrant country full of contrasts, colour and a wealth of design. You may feel apprehensive about using these designs in your home, so far away from their source, but you need not worry. All you need is a little bit of daring to carry it through.

Egypt holds a fascination for many people. Archaeologists have unearthed wonderful treasures to give us a picture of life in ancient Egypt and many exhibitions have toured the world showing us both the riches of the pharaohs and the simple utensils of the slaves.

The best place to start with a subject that is a little bit out of the ordinary is in a room that is either small or used exclusively by you and your family. The bathroom is a super room in which you

can be a little more exotic than usual. Paint your walls a delicate eau-de-Nil and stencil crossed palm leaves in different sizes in the top corners and let them filter onto the ceiling. Add a row of palm trees, interspersed with pyramids in a soft sandstone shade along the wall just above the tile level or at the height of the dado-rail.

If you are lucky enough to be the owner of a roll top, claw foot bath, continue the sandstone shade onto the sides and add the palm leaves, slightly scaled up, in a vibrant green brushed with gold. So, using just two designs and two basic colours you create a small leafy oasis in your own home.

Turn your attention to the bedroom. Fix a small shelf at each side of the bed instead of bedside tables. Against a background of light sandy yellow or reddish brown, stencil Egyptian figures, facing the bed, with an arm extended so as to appear to be holding the shelves aloft. Use black, white, turquoise and a pale sienna to colour the figures. Faux Arabic script in black or gold would make a marvellous wall or curtain border and a motif for a lampshade. If you want to give the room a really authentic Egyptian look, complete the decoration with an 'eye of Horus' on the wall over the bed to ward off evil spirits.

Your library will have books on travel, natural history and archaeology. You can make designs from a wide selection of gods, goddesses, temple dancers and acrobats. Look in the children's section of the library, as well, for more simplified drawings. The ancient Egyptians depicted themselves in a very naive, two dimensional manner, making them ideal subjects for stencilling. Hieroglyphics is the ancient form of writing using

*This is one of a pair of Egyptian ladies who reside at each end of the bath. The flickering candles lend a romantic touch to bath time.*

*The reed border winds lazily around the bathroom floor in shades of green and purple. These evocative colours blend beautifully with the stripped pine floor.*

*Fans, figures and palms adorn this trio of bolster cushions. Silks, satins and velvets in vibrant colours would be ideal materials to use.*

symbols instead of words for the text. You will easily find examples of this during your research. You could then try to form some text that has some special significance to you or your family. I have seen the word 'Cleopatra' spelled out in a reference book and you could easily stencil this on the wall over your bath for a conversation piece.

Look at ancient illustrations of gardens. You will see interior rectangles with the plants laid out flat along the outside edges. Stencil one of these as a border, changing the colours of the plants at every repeat, in your kitchen. It will look slightly geometric but with a charming simplicity. A water garden with reeds, rushes, lotus blossoms and ibis would be a little more unusual.

Terracotta is one of my favourite materials. It is also a natural support for stencilling. There are so many different pots around that you will easily find ones to suit your taste. Stencil directly onto the terracotta or paint the pots white first and colour-wash them with watered-down emulsion in really bright, vibrant colours.

Why not stencil a red coffee table with a row of camels strolling along the edges? You can use three different sizes of stencil for variety then embellish the legs of the table with a series of small motifs such as the ankh. Coffee tables are good subjects for newcomers to stencil. They are not so large as to be daunting and they have a flat surface. You can always start by painting and stencilling a piece of wood and making it into a coffee table later.

What colours do you think of in relation to Egypt? Naturally you will think of sandy yellows and the green of palm leaves. Now think a little deeper. There is the unmistakable blue of lapis lazuli, the fiery flash of sunset over the pyramids, the gold in Tutankhamun's mask and many more. You do not need to slavishly recreate an Egyptian room to evoke the spirit of the place; all you need to do is to use the correct colour scheme and stencil smaller items to provide atmosphere. Try papyrus lampshades, creamy blinds and a cotton bath mat. Using papyrus to be authentic, stencil a set of wall hangings or a bedcover in thick cotton.

Egypt's rulers always had slaves to cool them with huge decorative fans. Stencil your own fans over your bed in earthy colours such as ochre, umber and turquoise.

I have seen the most marvellous Egyptian light fitting. It is made of solid brass, has a filigree design cut into it and is studded with imitation glass jewels that shine in different colours when the light goes on. It would make the most exotic stencil for the hallway or a richly decorated bathroom. Design a group of three different lamps on the same theme and let them hang from thick-gold stencilled chains at differing height from the ceiling. They will create a wonderful Egyptian atmosphere.

You will be surprised at the wealth of reference material available to make designs on this theme. Go ahead, open a book and go to Egypt in your armchair.

*I found these clay pots in a garden centre, painted them with a white base then colour-washed them with watered down emulsion (latex) paint. The Egyptian motifs are an ideal finishing touch.*

*Place the seated lady on place mats in your dining room. You could make a marvellous themed dining room using the designs in this section. Just for fun, why not take the time to plan one? You may be so inspired you will put your ideas into practice.*

*The camel is a real piece of fun. Let him walk around your kitchen or stencil him onto tiles always facing the oasis of the taps. Colour the eye by hand.*

*All these figures are in the traditional style and can be stencilled as a sumptuous border in your hallway or delicately onto muslin curtains. Enlarge the figures to stand guard at your hallway doors or in the bathroom on either side of the bath. Make a second overlay for the lady's belt.*

The tree is a design taken from an illustration of an Egyptian garden. It is a naive design that could work equally well outside an Egyptian theme.

The pyramids can be stencilled in a very short time. Make the colour scheme really rich with orange, red and terracotta.

The ankh is the symbol of life. Use it on bedding or enlarged over your fireplace. Make a second stencil for the darkened area.

Use the eye of Horus as protection in your home. Cut a second stencil for the pupil.

The symbol similar to a twisted rope represents flax and makes a good fill-in design to mix into borders.

The scarab is a lucky charm in Egypt. Colour it in turquoise and verdigris on vases and jewellery boxes.

Reeds can be used as individual designs or in small bunches. Stencil them in blue and turquoise on kitchen doors or onto utensil and storage jars.

I am a true cat lover and this Egyptian cat is wonderful. The traditional colourway is black and I see no reason in this instance to change it. It would be marvellous stencilled onto the lower edges of your curtains or on your mantelpiece, one on either end.

The fan can be used for a border. Put fans in a line or invert every second motif or even stencil them in a pyramid shape. Red, yellow and cream would be interesting as would pink, silver and purple. You don't have to stick to typical colour schemes. That side of the job is entirely up to you.

The crossed palm leaves is a fairly traditional design and can be used in any room in the house. For a change, stencil in black and gold, navy blue and silver or orange and terracotta.

The horns containing circles are the symbol for eternity. This is a fantastic design to stencil on your bed head or hope chest.

# Chapter 2

# CHILDREN'S ROOM

*Adoring farm animals and clowns, cuddly kittens and puppies, spaceships and planets, insects and monsters: children are capable of great passions, some ephemeral, some durable. Each is of great interest until the next one comes along.*

PREVIOUS PAGE
*During the night the little mice come out to dance.*

ABOVE
*This wigwam has been stencilled with brightly coloured head dresses and arrows. You could also stencil flowers and grasses or small animals.*
Inset: *The feathers of the head-dress can be coloured differently on each repeat and used as a border.*

You will find that your child's hobbies and interests are the best starting points for your designs. The most obvious places for these designs are nurseries, playrooms or children's bedrooms. Bright colours or pastel hues to your child's taste are all perfectly in order. By involving your children in the decoration of their personal spaces you will stimulate their imagination and probably receive some very odd requests for stencils.

For the budding entomologist why not make a row of grasshoppers along the skirting board or leaping to different heights to make a growth chart? Miss Muffet's spider could hang by a single dark line overlooked by a flight of bats across the ceiling. These subjects, whilst perhaps not to your taste, could be very appealing to your children.

A child's collection would also make a good starting point. Stamps stencilled around a bed head or bursting out of a wall light would be entertaining. Piles of sea shells stencilled in lower corners of the room and then spilling onto the floor could either be lifelike or jazzily multi-coloured. Bright colours can also be brought into play by stencilling a mass of butterflies on the ceiling, gathering in greater numbers towards the light.

It doesn't matter if your child is interested in such diversities as dinosaurs and spaceships. You can incorporate both into a landscape with the dinosaurs

*Originally I planned four designs to be placed in cameos on the sides and lid of the toy box. Then imagination took over, and the dinosaurs found themselves in a landscape with trees, a lake and an erupting volcano. Apart from the initial base coat of paint, all the designs were produced using basic stencilling equipment.*

peering out of exotic undergrowth at spaceships flying through wispy clouds. You can put any combination of designs together with a little imagination.

A play room, especially if it is shared, can be divided by using stencils so that each child has its own clearly defined area. Toy boxes, desks and walls can all be personalised with any identifying device your child wants.

Huge floor cushions can be stencilled with huge favourite animals. Bean bags, stencilled with large teddy bears will hug your children and keep them warm. Sport is an important feature in many children's lives. Stencil surfboarders, ice skaters, footballers and even a border of colourful football-team strips. Cricket's natural elegance can produce a stunning border of batsmen and bowlers. Paint the room pale blue sponged with green up to dado-rail height and shape the edge to represent waves. Snorkellers could float around, peeping from behind brightly coloured coral whilst water-skiers make waves on the surface.

Send the owl and the pussycat out to sea in their beautiful pea-green boat. They could float gently along in a border or sit placidly in a larger mural over the bed head. Create a 'secret garden' especially for your own children or stencil large flower heads with little children sitting on the petals. Friendly cows, wearing battered hats, can stare over picket fences whilst fat brown hens peck at the skirting board.

Look to *The Arabian Nights* for inspiration where you will find flying carpets, the genie of the lamp and hidden treasures. What more could a child want? Stencil the carpet on the floor, the genie on the walls in brightly coloured robes and the treasure in chests along the skirting boards. Stencil a ballet scene or make a border from all the elements of the ballet that you can think of.

A fairy story will give you inspiration. You don't have to design the whole thing, just different motifs to give the gist of things. Your child will be able to

*Book-ends are the ideal spot for the flower children. They are easy to make and are an ideal starter project.*

fill in the gaps. How about Cinderella's coach and a glass slipper or Hansel and Gretel and a gingerbread house? Thumbelina would be pretty, flying with the swallow.

How about stencilling a chess and draughts board onto the floor. Make it any size you like but a larger design would be fun. Then stencil the chess pieces onto flat pieces of card, lightweight wood or even onto cushions.

Stencil a row of mushrooms and toadstools on the wall near floor level. Make tall ones and little dumpy ones, colouring them brightly and adding spots and stripes and any other motif you want. I would put little doors and windows in them and put fluorescent paint in some of the windows so that

they will glow in semi-darkness. The next step is to stencil the inhabitants of these little homes. If you stencil them onto balsa wood you can hang them on the walls so that they stand on the caps, lean against the stems or just walk from one home to another. These figures can be little animals, fairies or elves or you can even add the caterpillar from *Alice in Wonderland*. As these figures are separate from the main stencilling you can move them from one mushroom to another and if you hinge their limbs you can change their positions as well.

Stencil a large puppet with hinged limbs and hang it from the ceiling by strings. It need not be a person. It can be a teddy bear, a frog or anything that your child wants.

A screen is a good idea for a child's room as long as it is securely based so that it will not fall over. It will be a decorative feature and it will also hide a lot of clutter. Stencil it with an outdoor scene such as Ratty and Mole rowing down the river or a teddy bear's picnic. This also gives you the excuse to stencil food which seems to be a popular topic with children. For older children use sports scenes or ribbons, bows and flowers.

A tiny member of our family by the name of Holly is absolutely crazy about mermaids. They are a wonderful subject for stencilling. Sit them on rocks, have them combing their hair, splashing about on the surface of the water or swimming down in the depths to pick pearls from giant oysters. Iridescent colours for the tails will give a jewel-like finish. You can add little 'merbabies' having swimming lessons to the design.

Make a line of robots pace along the wall. There are lots of opportunities for bright colours here. Animal tracks will be educational and you can stencil them absolutely anywhere from the floor to the ceiling.

Children are interested in anything and everything so your only problem will be to narrow the choice of your designs down to just a hundred!

*ABOVE*

*An alcove with a built-in shelf is a show-piece for a small collection of doll's-house furniture with the stencilled town house as a delightful backdrop.*

*RIGHT*

*The totem 'pole' is made from several roughly cut pieces of calico tied together with string for a homespun look. This is a simple and inexpensive way to add decoration to any room in the house.*

The dancing mice would be ideal for a toy box or a bed head. Stencil them onto a mobile to make them dance. Make a separate overlay for pockets, buttons and whiskers.

This little girl and her pony could trot around walls, curtains and cupboard doors. Modify the basic design to make the pony go over jumps. Make a separate overlay for the darkened areas.

Sport is always popular with older children. For the ball, cut a separate overlay for the stitching and use the design in a border or mixed with other sportsmen.

27

Prehistoric beasties are endlessly fascinating to children. The colours you use are unimportant but try to get your children to pick their own. Stencil these designs into just one corner of the room near the floor and use the flying reptiles on a lampshade.

Pussycats are always a favourite amongst children. Use either natural colours or go for something different using pinks, blues and purples. Stencil the cat peering through the grass or standing on a fence.

Indian designs can be stencilled as a border or onto Indian costumes. Cut a second overlay for the darkened areas.

A jack-in-a-box is ideal for a brightly coloured border. Use a separate overlay for the facial features and the box decoration. The doll's house is a pretty subject for a border or a bedcover. Carefully work out how many overlays you will need to cut.

The pansy girl and daisy boy can be used as a pair or apart. Make separate overlays for the facial features, pockets, buttons and pansy centre.

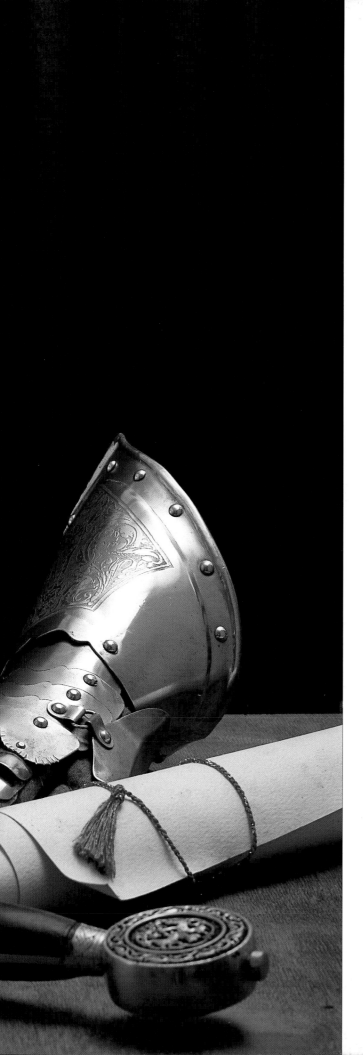

# Chapter 3

# PERIOD LIVING

*Swoon to heraldic beasts, shields and armour, musical scores and flowing lines of poetry, hedges trimmed into fantastic shapes, glowing stained glass, complex wood carvings and Celtic braids. Whether you live in a period or a modern home you will find something in these designs to suit your lifestyle.*

*PREVIOUS PAGE*
*These wonderful, creamy candles are the perfect foil for gold sprayed motifs and would make a wonderful centrepiece for a themed dinner party.*

*ABOVE*
*A border of fleur-de-lis in differing sizes makes a marvellous backdrop to the dark walls and furniture.*

Do you have a favourite fragment of poetry? Find a calligraphic alphabet that pleases you and make the stencils you need for your poem. Either cut the poem in one whole stencil or make separate letters. Place a romantic poem on the wall over your bed or on the ceiling, either in one colour to blend in with your decorative scheme or in bright colours. Make small designs to illustrate the poem and stencil them on your bed hangings or draped muslin curtains. Set the poem around a picture frame or mirror. Add inspirational prose to a study or workroom whilst humorous lines would work in a playroom or dining room.

Liven up an unattractive view with a stencilled stained-glass design on your window. Flowers, birds and landscapes are all possible as are more modern scenes such as golfers or fishermen. Use brilliantly coloured, transparent glass paints or use frosted glass spray to imitate an etched design. You can also paint this afterwards with subtle colours.

You could stencil a suit of armour into a corner of your hallway. Armour is modular and converts easily into stencil form. Alternatively, just stencil different pieces of armour into a border. Smaller knights could sit astride their suitably caparisoned chargers in a border in your hallway. Give them lances and they could joust, in pairs, on your stair risers.

Heraldic designs are ideal for use in a study or den. Use them on the walls and curtains and also on letter racks, desks and stationery.

The English rose is a very popular subject. Stencil it in 3D on the panels of your doors or onto an old chest to place on the floor at the end of your bed. Make a coronet in MDF for your bed hangings, stencil it with the roses and intersperse them with stuck-on glass jewels.

In heraldry, not only the positioning of the elements has a distinct meaning but the colours are specific and have meaning too. You can abide by the rules or go with your own colour schemes.

Look at columns, finials, architrave and, just for fun, gargoyles, as children will love them. You could stencil Gothic archways in your hallway. They don't

*The wide ribbon tie-backs are stencilled with the Celtic braid to match the edge of the hangings. This is a simple method of co-ordinating your decorations.*

*I just love this curvy metal lamp. Blue and gold make an interesting colour scheme for the heraldic lion and small fleur-de-lis.*

OPPOSITE

*A cold white bathroom was transformed with a terracotta colour-wash. Ivy and Celtic designs in shades of green are a wonderful contrast on the walls and provide a softer effect on the muslin hanging.*

*This is a crisp, contrasting colour scheme for a cache pot. The green, gold and black are a perfect counterfoil for most leafy plants.*

have to be black and dismal, you could use warm stone colours instead.

Stencil metallic wall sconces on your chimney breast and adorn them with white lilies. Make a lily and ivy border around a pale-green living room just below the ceiling with a black lily border on curtain tie-backs.

Medieval tapestries are another source of inspiration, including figures, trees, harts and doves. Make your own wall hangings using knights, unicorns, and medieval ladies, and a border of flowing lilies. Single items from the hanging could then be stencilled onto cushions with tasselled corners. If you stencil

using a pouncing method you can give them something of the effect of tapestry.

Mythical beasts – Dragons, griffins and flying horses – all have their place here.

Celtic design is enjoying a revival. Look at the *Book of Kells* and medieval carvings. Some lines form patterns of birds, animals and flowers, whilst others meander, forming complex designs. Imagine a floor bordered with wide Celtic braid and a complex motif in the centre. Use whatever colours you want.

Once you get used to the idea that your home can indeed be your castle, I am sure that you will use these ideas and more with great enthusiasm.

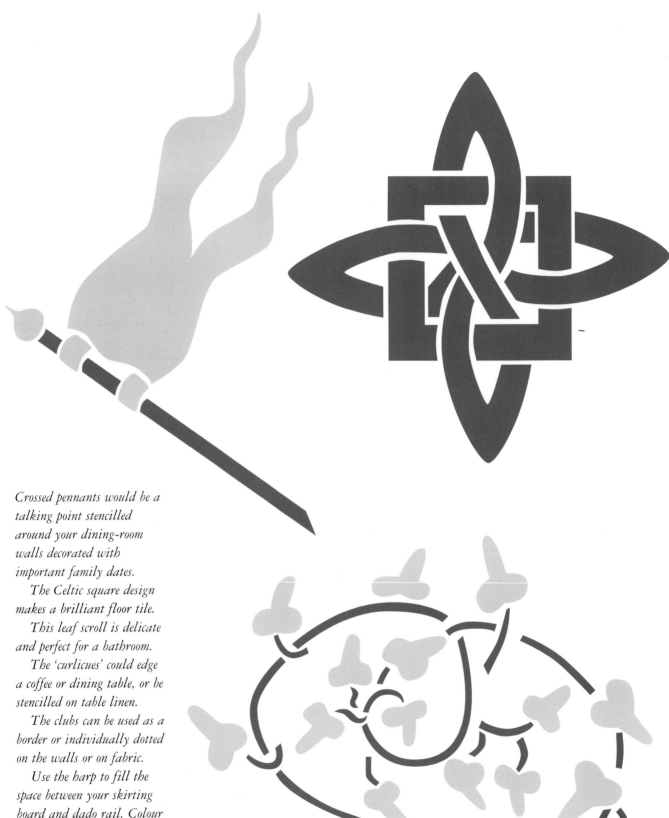

Crossed pennants would be a talking point stencilled around your dining-room walls decorated with important family dates.

The Celtic square design makes a brilliant floor tile.

This leaf scroll is delicate and perfect for a bathroom.

The 'curlicues' could edge a coffee or dining table, or be stencilled on table linen.

The clubs can be used as a border or individually dotted on the walls or on fabric.

Use the harp to fill the space between your skirting board and dado rail. Colour the string by hand.

Stencil the topiary pot on a grand scale at either side of your door or use it in the kitchen or in a child's room. Cut a second overlay for the decoration on the pot.

Bed hangings or a canopy would be the perfect spot to stencil the crown design.

Ivy designs are among my favourites as they are so versatile.

The traditional English rose would look wonderful in red, green and gold.

Add the heraldic lion to the shield or stencil it onto the backrest of your dining chairs.

The scroll can contain family names or a house name. Stencil it over your fire place or on the wall over your bed.

Stencil the double swirl around the edges of your curtains or as a border instead of a dado rail.

A B C D E
F G H I J
K L M N O
P Q R S T
U V W X Y
Z 1 2 3 4 5 6
7 8 9 0

*The alphabet and numbers can be used for stencilling Gothic script around your home and to personalise your belongings.*

What could be prettier than a fleur-de-lis stencilled onto a draped muslin curtain? Apply the design in black for a wonderful gothic feel.

Give yourself a coat of arms by adding personal designs or initials to the shield, or use it to create a multi-coloured border. Make as many overlays as you need for your colour scheme.

The stone cross would look marvellous as a border in a reading room.

You could stencil the flowing armlet design onto the wall around your bed head, around picture frames or onto the wall around your bathroom mirror.

# Chapter 4

# NATURE TRAIL

*Birds fluttering through the rainforest
or in formation over misty fens, jewelled
fish darting through crystal clear waters
and tadpoles in a jam jar, lizards
scampering over sun drenched rocks and
bees buzzing around the flowers on a
summer's day all look delightful. If you
are thrilled by nature in all its forms
you will enjoy bringing a wealth of
stencilled wildlife into your home.*

PREVIOUS PAGE

*A plain yellow living room looks tranquil with its border of leaves in autumn colours. The cut-out leaves have been used to produce reverse stencilling on some of the leaf motifs dotted around the walls.*

BELOW

*This room belongs to a young scuba diver who adores the water. She is delighted with her aquatic bedroom where the fish fly and the waves break lazily along the walls.*

If you live in the countryside you won't have to look far for inspiration for wonderful designs from nature. For the town-dweller a trip to the library or a long walk in the park with a sketchbook will prove invaluable. Magazines, trips to the zoo, botanical gardens and arboretums are ideal sources. Designing a stencil from a favourite flower discovered on a holiday will be a source of happy memories for years to come.

Select your five favourite wild flowers. Stencil each one in rotation as a border in your kitchen. It doesn't matter if they are of different heights and widths as this will help to add interest. Using ceramic paints, stencil them onto randomly selected tiles. Then create a

special design using all five flowers to use as a motif on doors. Stencil all five in a row, fix a hook onto the wall under each one to hang a set of wooden spoons or pot cloths, also stencilled to match.

Still in the kitchen, devise a summer landscape on the blind with leafy branches, birds and egg-filled nests. Don't just think of local birds; stencil toucans, parrots and lovebirds. Autumn leaves in bronze, gold and copper metallic paints would look luxurious.

The dining room is another area where you can expand your creative talents. Stencil a set of place mats, each with a different animal or bird bordered by grasses and leaves. In a minimalist scheme stencil each mat with the pattern

of a different animal skin such as tiger and leopard. If you are feeling really adventurous you could stencil the table itself with a jungle scene.

Your bedroom would be transformed by a host of tropical birds. Paint your walls in dreamy pastel shades and adorn the walls with climbing flowers, perhaps trumpet vines, in pink and pale coral. Hovering hummingbirds in vibrant colours dotted around the room would draw the eye and excite the senses.

Decorate mirror glass or mirror tiles with swans and watery ripples. Use etching spray, leave the ripples unpainted but colour the swans in white. Paint them black for a dramatic effect.

For the bathroom, etched seashells on your window would ensure privacy and you could change the colours whenever you changed your decor. A swag or garland of sea shells with sea horses would be very unusual and would work in the bathroom or the bedroom.

Many people would consider stencilling a border or tie-backs but why not whole curtains? You could use one huge, detailed stencil of an eagle and clouds, then, when you close the curtains, the decoration would appear.

Peacocks are the most beautiful birds. You can make a stencil as complex or as simple as you like. Use the stencil in the hallway as a border at dado height

*A mixture of designs has been used on these tiles to show you what different effects you can achieve. The dolphin and waves and the parrot have been decorated with the three dimensional medium before painting, whilst the rest have been painted with hobby ceramic colours.*

*The hawk stencil was fixed securely to the glass and sprayed with glass etching spray. This gave the frosted appearance which has been left unpainted to give the effect of clouds. The stencil was left in place and the rest of the design was coloured using oil paint sticks and a stencil brush.*

and fill in underneath to the skirting with stencils of individual feathers, randomly placed and angled. Natural colours would be bright but black and gold peacocks would be very dramatic. Imagine a mosaic peacock design on the floor of your hallway. That is an idea with instant impact.

Trees form a wonderful array of shapes, sizes and colours. They range from the vibrant reds of the maple, the golden orange of liquidamber to the soft green of the willow. Leaf shapes are a gift

to the stenciller, they are round, smooth, deeply etched or palmate. So, what can you do with these delights? I love muslin and voile panels. Stencil them with individual leaves so that when they are caught by a breeze the leaves will appear to tumble around the window or your bed. Make a mobile of stencilled tree shapes or leaves and hang it in your window. You could take this idea one step further: pick a tree and construct a mobile consisting of the tree shape to hang centrally, some leaves in summer and autumn clothing, and its flowers and fruits. You could have the main support in the form of the letters spelling out the name of the tree. This would make a wonderful, unusual gift. Just think how many other subjects would respond to this treatment.

Fossils are another source of interest. The shapes are simple to copy and a large ammonite would be an unusual decoration for a study.

A collection of big cats on your living room cushions would be stunning. Try lions, panthers, tigers and leopards. Stencil a cat as the decoration on a letter rack. Stencil two lions, each on a separate piece of wood and each facing inwards. These will form book-ends and will look even better when you cut around the edges of the stencilling with a jigsaw. A collection of primates could adorn the floor cushions in a young person's room and a large, ginger orang-utan could sit atop the door frame.

Encourage your children's interest in natural history by getting them to make a collection of pictures of rare animals, birds and flowers. You can then get together and make stencils for school projects. A stencilled diary of local flora would be very interesting to undertake and could become a treasured heirloom.

If you have a specific interest, be it flowers or fish or bird life, you can find inspiration for stencil designs to use in your home. If everyone in your family has a different interest you will find that your stencilling skills are always on call.

*This box was a junk shop purchase. I painted over the gingham check covering with several coats of paint and glaze then added the hummingbird and vibrant hibiscus. The matching ribbon completes the picture.*

these three little
bathroom
windows or on bath panels.
Cut the full shape and the
stripes as separate overlays.
Use the coral as a border
to complement the fish.

A delightful dolphin
leaps between gigantic
waves. Make one large
stencil and put it on the
wall along the long side of
your bath.

Stencil the chameleon
in the same colour as its
background like a real
chameleon. Pearlised spray
paints are ideal. Cut a
second stencil for the line on
the tail and the features,
or colour them by hand.

Stencil the grasshopper
in bright leaf green.

Dragonflies dart along
the surface of water so
stencil them in your
bathroom on towels, and
on and around mirrors.

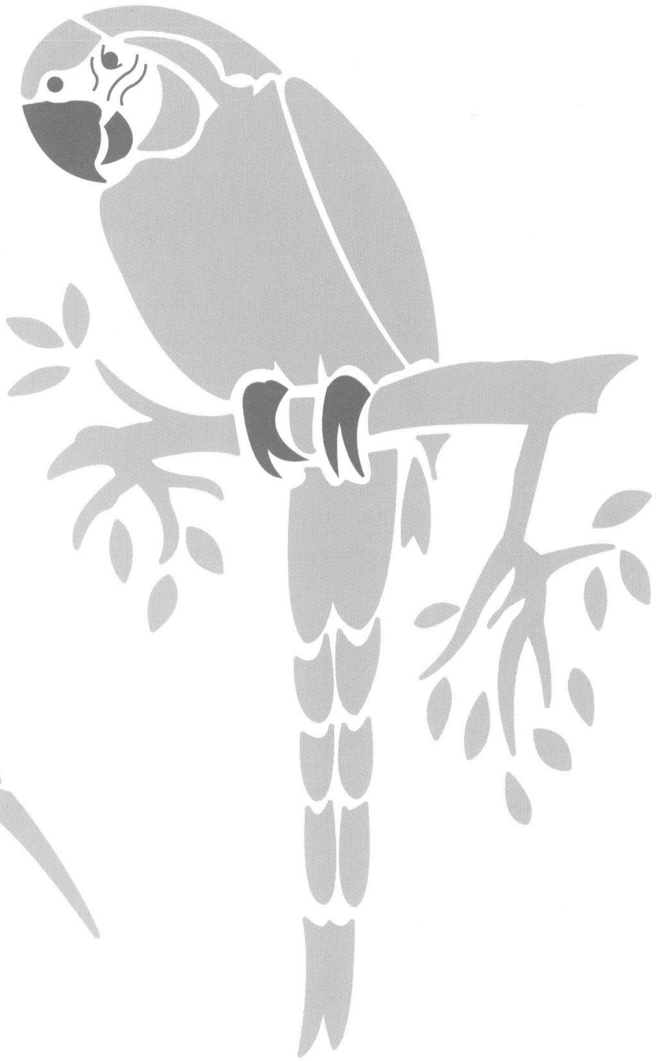

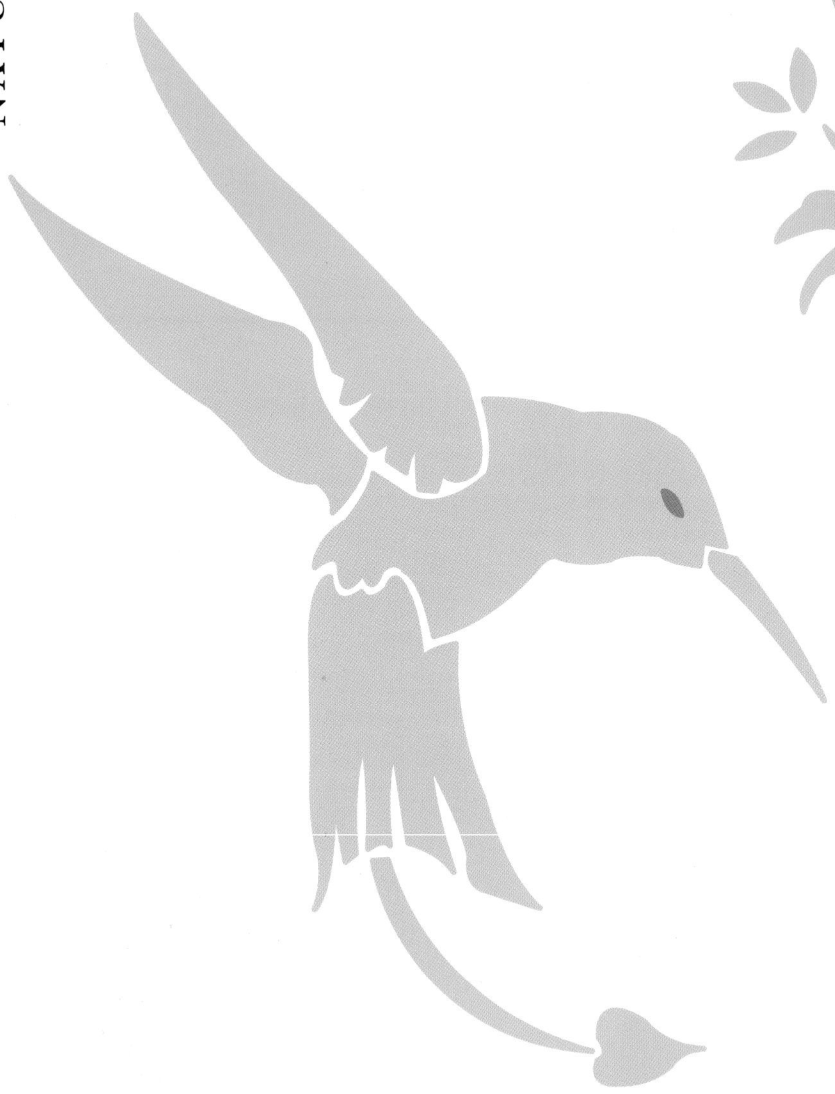

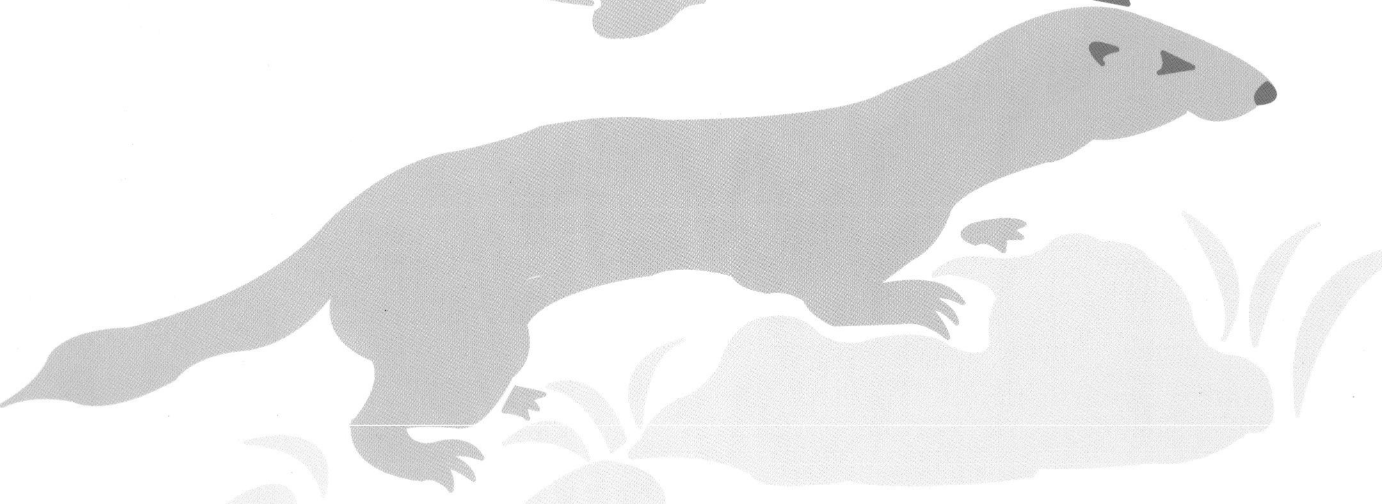

The parrot would be perfect
perched in a garden room or
conservatory.

Stencil a small group of
hummingbirds on the wall
around where you normally
place a vase of flowers.
Colour the eyes by hand.

The weasel could join a
collection of small animals on
seat cushions. Make separate
overlays for each shade.

The turtle would be
interesting in a study or as a
large motif in a playroom.

Stencil the hawk on a fire
screen, on a vase or as a large
motif on a screen. Make a
second overlay for the eye.

53

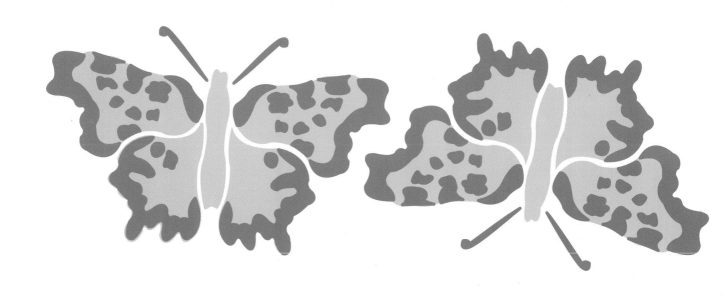

Cut two overlays for the butterfly, the body and wings on the first and the decorative detail on the second. Colour them red and black, blue and purple or pale lemon and green.

Stencil the orchids on a swirl of fabric twisted around a curtain pole. Black and gold on cream would be stunning or blue and lilac would be pretty.

Bright pink or pastel would be perfect for this hibiscus but why not try yellow or orange? It would be wonderful in a breakfast room climbing around the windows or on a painted wall in your garden. Cut a separate overlay for the petal and leaf patterns.

Try the leaves border in your kitchen above your tiles and around the windows. Put individual leaves on your tiles. Make a second overlay for the leaf pattern.

# Chapter 5

# MYSTIC HORIZONS

*Candles; stars, suns and moons; chimes; windows draped with floating fabrics in jewel colours; many faceted crystals; and healing signs can all evoke a sense of peace and harmony to help you unwind at the end of a busy day.*

PREVIOUS PAGE
*This zodiac wheel was created using individual pie slices, each stencilled with a different star sign, then pieced together to make this wonderful centrepiece. You do not have to make a wheel. Stencil the designs into squares on a coffee table or on the tiles in your bathroom.*

*The coffee table with its sun, moons and stars would take on a whole new mood if it was painted cream and finished with gold stencilling.*

In these days of stresses and pressures there is a never-ending search for a better life. Perhaps in this chapter, you will find some ideas to bring tranquillity to your days. The colours that you use can be calm pastels or vibrant, ostentatious colours such as purples and magentas.

I adore candles. Their tiny flickering flames are truly romantic and cast such a gentle glow around the room. Place a crowd of smooth, fat candles on a table top. Use different shapes and sizes and put them on a variety of holders. If you stencil more candles in the background and colour the flames in metallic paints you can make this crowd of candles look much larger. A pair of large church candles in candlesticks would look very imposing at either side of your dining-room door. Use different shades of white, coffee and cream for the sticks and bright red for the candles.

Paint your walls a rich, deep blue and spray stencil a mass of silver stars in an arching border from the ceiling down. If you leave some areas only lightly dusted with stars you can fill them with moons, each one in a different phase. Make your stars different shapes and sizes; some with straight edges, some wiggly; and give them a variety of spikes.

Your stars need not be silver. Make them pink, purple and lilac or jade green, turquoise and ultramarine. Just pick your favourite colour scheme.

The sun is another popular motif. Gold suns would be beautiful on festoon blinds or on a pelmet. Black suns and stars are a wonderfully Gothic idea. A mosaic sun design stencilled onto your garden table and seat cushions or deckchair covers would be very original. You will be surprised at how many different sun motifs you can think of. Pick out the ones you like best and, using tracing paper, try out different ways of using them. Cut them in half to make

staggered borders, make a circle of suns or put them into the spaces between Regency stripes. This is a good exercise to try with any design. Experiment with pencils, scissors and paper and use coloured pencils to test your colour schemes. It is fun to do and you will find out how creative you really are.

Traditional Romanies have a mystical reputation. Create a gypsy theme in your bedroom with floaty fabrics, stencilled with stars and planets. Add stencilled tarot designs interspersed with crystal balls to the walls.

The zodiac signs make wonderful stencils and you can make them in any style you want. You don't have to make a full set, just make the ones relevant to your family and stencil them onto their

*This is a simple border made up of candlesticks, lightning and crystal balls. Varying the sizes of the candles and their colours makes a bright feature. It would look even more sophisticated with gold candlesticks, creamy candles, silver balls and black lightning.*

*An old jewellery box that had seen better days was stripped, sanded, painted with a wash then decorated with stars and the Aquarius motif. These zodiac designs are an unusual way to personalise a special gift.*

bedroom doors or in a border over their beds. Just for fun you could stencil the whole family's star signs onto a house name or number sign or even onto your post-box. Stencil them onto tiles in your kitchen or onto the underside of the glass of a coffee table.

A really big project would be to stencil a zodiac wheel onto a wooden floor. This would be wonderful in a dining room especially if teamed with the stars and moons idea suggested earlier.

Add Japanese zodiac signs to an oriental room or planet signs to a hallway. Paint your ceiling black or purple then stencil constellations, joining the stars with straight grey lines. Name

them with calligraphic scripts in glittering gold spray paint.

A shop near to our home sells magic wands made to a special formula. Stencilled wands in bright colours would make a delightful border, especially if sprinkled with fairy dust. For a really ostentatious look use stick-on glass jewels and for the fairy dust use glitter from a craft shop.

There are many subjects in this section that would make wonderful mobiles. Of those already mentioned, the sun, moon and stars is an obvious theme but try crystals, constellations and zodiacs. Not so obvious are healing plants and colour-therapy shades.

*These inexpensive gift-shop shelves were sanded down, painted with a small pot of craft glaze and adorned with stars to make a perfect setting for the fantasy figures.*

I have a set of chimes in my workroom near the window. If the breeze does not set them going then the cat will, as she finds them endlessly fascinating. There are chimes set in spirals, circles and horizontal lines. They are multicoloured, metallic, pottery or natural bamboo. Stencil yourself a range of chimes to make a high border in your garden room or entrance hall then mix in as many real chimes as you want.

Temple bells are another design theme for you to follow to use in the bedroom or bathroom.

There are many mysterious places on the planet to give you inspiration. Stonehenge is perhaps the best example. Make a design of a stone circle and at each repeat stencil the sun or the moon and stars above it's centre point. Why not stencil a fairy ring instead with brightly coloured mushrooms and an ethereal fairy about to land?

This is a chapter where you can let your imagination soar. You can use colour-therapy techniques to exhilarate or soothe, and choose your favourite area of fantasy to enhance your life pattern.

61

I had tremendous fun making these zodiac signs. They are such mystical subjects that there are no barriers as to colour schemes. Many of them can be used as motifs outside the range of this chapter too. The fish for example would be suitably at home in a bathroom and the lion in a masculine bedroom. Make separate overlays for all the darkened areas, such as the fishes eyes and the star on the crab's back.

A lightning stencil would be fun crackling on the walls around your stereo system.

Mix and match these candle designs with the holders and make your own candle shapes as well; black holders with white candles look superb.

Yin Yang symbols would be an amazing addition to a simple bedroom. Make two overlays for this design.

You can make this delicate sun any size you want. Stencil a large motif in gold on your kitchen cupboards and run a tiny sun along your shelf edges.

The moon and stars would look pretty on a glass light shade or placed in a regular pattern above a dado rail.

Why not stencil these stars on a ceiling. Silver stars on a maroon ground would look stunning in the dining room.

The crystal ball can be difficult to cut so use a plate as a template.Change the stand size by photocopying up or down. Cut a second overlay for the highlight.

Shooting stars can tumble down your walls from the ceiling. Stencil them in droves.

# Chapter 6

# FIGURATIVELY SPEAKING

*Dancers from around the world, Art Deco and Art Nouveau figurines, historical figures with flowing robes, tiny tots and humorous characters are all suitable subjects for your home. Stencil them large and small in simple or complex patterns. This is a complete change of subject from the usual flora and once it captures your interest you won't want to stop.*

71

PREVIOUS PAGE
*The flowing lines and subtle colours of this charming border are peaceful, harmonious and form a perfect setting for a totally feminine room.*

ABOVE
*The owner of this bathroom wanted cherubs on her walls to complement the cherubs on the tile design. Blue on blue is very peaceful and the cherubs float happily around the room both in a border and as motifs.*

The human form is the most popular subject for artists and photographers alike. There is a never ending interest in other people and their lives.

Sumo wrestlers, and other martial artists make ideal subjects for stencil design. Stencil TaeKwonDo figures at the peak of a flying kick or stencil a figure completing a pattern of set moves. This will make both a perfect border and point of reference for the budding martial artist.

Look at ancient Greek vases decorated with graceful robed figures dancing around the sides. Single figures as motifs in a dining room and on curtains would be luxurious, especially in gold and earthy reds on a cream ground. Stencil statues standing on small columns as well. Stencil them in their original bright colours or in greys, marbles and stone colours as they are now.

Dancers are a wonderful stencil theme. Irish dancing is very much in vogue. The dancers are lithe and graceful and for teenage rooms they would be ideal. A row of kicking dancers interspersed with Celtic braid designs is a lovely idea. Change the dancers to a line of can-can ladies and you have a totally different look. Ballet dancers are always a favourite as are traditional Balinese and Thai dancers in their wonderful costumes. Isadora Duncan's flowing gowns and scarves are a marvellous subject for stencil design.

You can design characters from opera, musical theatre, fiction and film. A border made up of the characters from *Pride and Prejudice* would be lovely. Why not try a border of a set of fictional detectives ranging from medieval to modern times?

Pick out a period of history that appeals to you. Naval officers from the past and ship's signal flags would be perfect for a young person who wanted to sail the seas. Spacemen are for those with loftier ideas.

Fashion models are ideal for a sewing room where each model can take on a different look or wear different clothes from the same decade.

Stencil busts of famous composers and writers for a music or reading room ,adding quotations and musical notes.

Your stencilled figures could take up your family's hobbies: gardeners with giant-sized flowers and fruit; artists with colourful palettes; or photographers standing on curling rolls of film.

Your children may appreciate some characters from children's fiction, fairy tales and adventure stories.

Star-crossed lovers such as Romeo and Juliet or Tristan and Isolde would

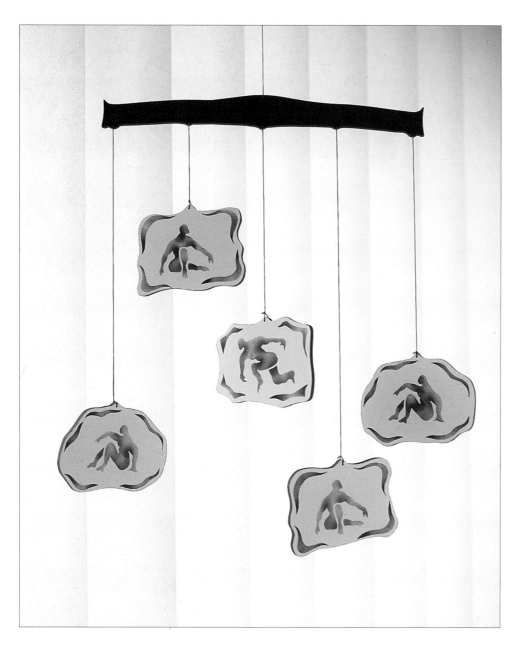

*This is a simple project for the new stenciller. The simple figures were stencilled onto MDF and cut out using a jigsaw. A hole was drilled into each one and they were strung onto this home-made support. With the uncluttered design and easy colours it is a perfect decorative feature for a modern study.*

OPPOSITE
*The charming Deco dancer weaves her way around this frosted glass vase. Another colour scheme, perhaps black and gold, would give a totally different look.*

RIGHT
*This is an example of how to take a motif, here the Flora figure, and by adding a variety of extra elements, in this case flowers and ribbons, make a truly stunning design. The robed lady could also be used in this manner, perhaps with grapes and urns as the additional material.*

be romantic. On the other hand Laurel and Hardy may be more to your taste.

Mythology is another fine source. Illustrate Narcissus admiring himself in the pool, Pandora opening the box or the moon spinners of ancient Greece.

Look at the work of famous artists such as Reubens, Gaugin and Lautrec for inspiration. A tastefully stencilled nude in the bathroom would be terrific. Colour the figure in misty white like a Lalique figure on a blue background.

A Victorian lady in a large hat and bustle would be very amusing if stencilled in profile and followed by a train of children of ever-diminishing size.

Ceramics is another area to look into. Shepherds, shepherdesses and milkmaids will suit a farmhouse kitchen whilst cameo figures in oval frames would be perfect in a sophisticated bedroom.

For a 1920's dining room, design a series of flappers, in swinging beaded dresses, dancing the Charleston or ballroom dancers executing a tango.

Look to foreign shores for belly dancers, exquisite geisha girls and Indian ladies in their scintillating saris.

You do not have to design a really complicated figure to get your meaning across. Start with simple stick figures. A group of these in a variety of poses would also make a simple but effective stencil.

People are endlessly fascinating and you only have to look around you to find the inspiration you need.

*Cherubs are an ever popular motif. One of these looks a little bit cheeky and would be super in the nursery. The other looks more serious. Add him to mirror frames and have him holding up your favourite pictures. If they are too heavy for a single cherub to hold, stencil two cherubs.*

*The deco dancer is so graceful and could easily decorate a light shade or a set of hatboxes. Be dramatic with navy blue and gold or iridescent fuchsia and orange.*

*Hawaiian dancers would look lovely swaying around a garden room. Reverse the design at every second repeat to give them movement.*

*The Flora design is a symbol of spring. Dress her in greens, yellows and blues and surround her with a circle of seasonal flowers either real or stencilled.*

Aren't these old fashioned bathers fun? He could have a costume of red with black stripes or light and dark blue. She could be pretty in pink and cream or dramatic in navy blue and white. Stencil them onto a mirror surround or onto your blinds. Make one extra overlay for the stripes of his costume and his moustache.

The flowing lines of the nouveau head form one of my favourite designs. She is superb as a large border at dado-rail height. Make a smaller border at picture-rail height and add her to your picture frames. Two large motifs with one reversed and offset would make a stunning centrepiece to your duvet cover and smaller heads could embellish your pillowcases.

The golfers are ideal for a study. Stencil them onto walls, light shades and box files in clear bright colours.

Let the skier slalom her way down the walls in a play room or stencil her onto sports bags.

The three Matisse figures
are a border in themselves or
use them individually.

The jolly lady would
look good in a child's room.
Make a separate overlay for
her buttons and shoes.

The crinoline lady is
every little girl's princess.
Make a second stencil for
the hair bow.

The deco lady could be
stencilled onto hairbrushes
or a jewellery box.

Stencil the water carrier
onto your curtains with
swirls of blue and green
flowing water.

The Roman lady would
make a wonderful border.
Make a second overlay for
the jewellery.

81

# Chapter 7

# TUTTI-FRUTTI

*Orchards in autumn and freshly
baked fruit pies, jams, jellies, berries and
hips, the perfect taste of strawberries and
cream, the bloom on a bunch of warm
grapes: there is such a richness in the
fruits of nature that your imagination
will run riot.*

*The screen was painted red then lilac, crackle glazed and decorated with the stencilled fruit bowl, swags and berry motifs. I put a relief stencil paste through the stencil with a palette knife, then, when the paste was dry, replaced the stencil and applied the colours.*

ABOVE
*Berries scramble along the dado-rail, around the mirror and make stylish motifs in the corners.*

Today, with imports from all over the world there is a wealth of fruit to choose from. There are so many weird and wonderful fruit shapes that you will have no trouble assembling enough samples to create an exotic fruit border.

Ripe figs, fresh from the tree, not only taste wonderful but they are such a marvellous 'saggy' shape. They make an interesting border coloured in mellow shades of green and purple. Mix them with ivy and olives and you have something really special to give your room a Mediterranean feel.

Stencil warm, soft peaches in natural colours onto a rust-red background in a dining room. Give them an authentic velvety texture by stippling the colours and enhance the effect by stencilling the leaves in smooth iridescent green.

Make swags of fruit, perhaps apples, pears and grapes and stencil them in your hallway as imitation corbels. Colour them as natural fruits or just use grey, black and stone colours to imitate plaster work.

Strawberries are the very essence of summer picnics on the lawn. As a stencil I think they work best as a delicate design. You can stencil them onto trays, tray cloths and napkins and onto the small beaded cloth covers that are used to drape over jugs of cool lemonade. Mix them with blueberries and blackberries for a pretty border in the kitchen and make circlets of the design for your tiles.

Blueberries are so appealing. Make little clumps of berries within a circle of leaves, create a curvy, sinuous trail or run the berries and leaves in a mock Regency stripe on your bedroom walls. One tiny berry with two tiny leaves would make a splendid motif for your voiles.

The fire screen at the beginning of this chapter is going to be used for an entirely different purpose. I am going to decorate my kitchen in a Mediterranean mix of lavender, with MDF cupboard doors colour-washed in light terracotta. Then, on the single blank wall I am going to fix the fire screen as a triptych. It will look absolutely stunning.

This is an idea that you can adapt to suit your own kitchen. You don't have to make a triptych. You can stencil small plaques and cut around the edges with a jigsaw. Cut lots of small squares and stencil them with the tiny fruit squares in the design pages. You can then stick the squares in a line on the front edges of a set of shelves. There are lots of ways you can use these techniques to brighten up your kitchen without spending a fortune. You could think big and make a large stencil of a cornucopia for a really impressive 3D panel on your larder door.

Grapes are always popular with the stenciller as their shape lends itself to stencil design. Make curvaceous bunches of fruit and colour them in purples and

*A border of grapes, apples, pears and blossom gives a bright colourful finish to this kitchen. Different segments of the border have been put together to form the randomly placed motifs.*

*Plums, cherries and ribbon work well together on this tablecloth. The napkins are decorated with the same border adapted to fit the smaller shape.*

greens or a sumptuous mix of the two. Make stylised bunches in a triangular or square shape but leaving the fruits curvy except on the outer edges. These would fit a modern kitchen very nicely as they are similar to checks but much more interesting.

Look around at the hedgerows. Hawthorn has wonderfully shaped leaves and the most beautiful vibrant fruits. Again, I think that delicacy is best here. Random leaves and berries in a border being blown by the wind is a super idea. Take a tip from cartoonists

and add a curvy line or two to the border to give the effect of movement.

Slice some fruits in half and you will get more ideas for stencil designs. Look at the watermelon with its wonderful colourful flesh, the kiwi fruit is a stunning green and black whilst the pomegranate is full of small ruby segments. Make borders of individual fruits or use a mixture for a really vibrant border.

Apples are not just green or red. Take a look at a fruit catalogue and you will see there is a wealth of colour in just one apple let alone in all the different varieties. Stencil one huge apple on the wall in your kitchen. It will test your powers of stencilling to create a truly life-like picture but just think how beautiful it will look when it is on the kitchen wall. Stencil a basket of apples with some over-spilling to form a border.

Pears could be stencilled to form a circle or mix them with pear blossom for place mats.

A mixed border of rare apples and pears, again mixed with blossoms, would be interesting to make, especially if you named the varieties in an ancient sepia script. Look at old volumes of botanical prints for inspiration here. Instead of using these designs as a border you could use them as pictures on your kitchen walls, still with the script, and each one framed with either real or stencilled gold frames. With a lick of paint and a new set of designs you could then change your gallery at very little cost.

These designs would look marvellous stencilled in transparent glass paints in the glass panels of interior doors or on the glass panel over a front door.

Tiles stencilled with fruits, especially in 3D, are a great idea fitted onto a fire-surround. You can then change the tiles when you change your colour scheme.

A simple border to make would be of naive trees with just dots of colour to represent fruit. This would look good anywhere in the house but especially in the hallway.

Stencil small fruit tarts on a tray, each one with a swirl of cream, and make a large lattice pie design as a centrepiece. Make a terrine of fruit with striped colours to represent the different fruits or put little arms and legs on the fruits, having them running around the walls.

Gardening books, plant catalogues and the supermarket are good points of reference for all these designs. All you have to do is look around you.

*Imagine taking this little basket with you into the countryside to collect fruits and berries for jams and pies.*

Stencil the berry cluster randomly or in vertical lines above and below a dado rail.

Checks, apples and pears would look pretty along the top of your kitchen tiles. Use the checks alone around door frames and light switches.

Stencil the apples onto your tablecloth and napkins and plain tea towels.

Colour the berries and leaves red, blue, orange or purple in a bright border or try peaceful blue in a bedroom.

The hips would look lovely around a mirror or light shade. Add them to a wooden floor and up the stairs.

The mixed fruit swag would look wonderful on door panels or as an edging for curtains. You will need more than one overlay.

88

Stencil this wonderful fruit bowl in the kitchen. It would also make an impressive border in a dining room. Colour it in shades of blue on a white ground. Cut as many overlays as you need.

Jam pots and fruit will give a lovely country feel to your home.

Fruit slices can be coloured orange, yellow and green for a citrus fruit border. Make a separate overlay for the pips.

The strawberry, cherry and blackberry squares could decorate jars of home-made jam, either directly onto the glass or onto sticky labels. Try other motifs with the square borders.

The cherry circle was designed to decorate tiles, glass vases and plates. You do not have to stick to red cherries, use pinks blended into yellow or black with deep purple and use a mixture of greens for the stems and leaves.

Just imagine the number of colour combinations you can think of for the plum and cherry border with its swirling ribbon. Use it just below the ceiling level in your dining room or kitchen and back to back over a doorway. Make a second overlay for the plum stripe.

Try stencilling the pineapple onto place mats or as a novel border in your hallway. You can use it with or without the small stand but you can use the stand stencil to hold other fruits or vegetables to create a link in a mixed border.

93

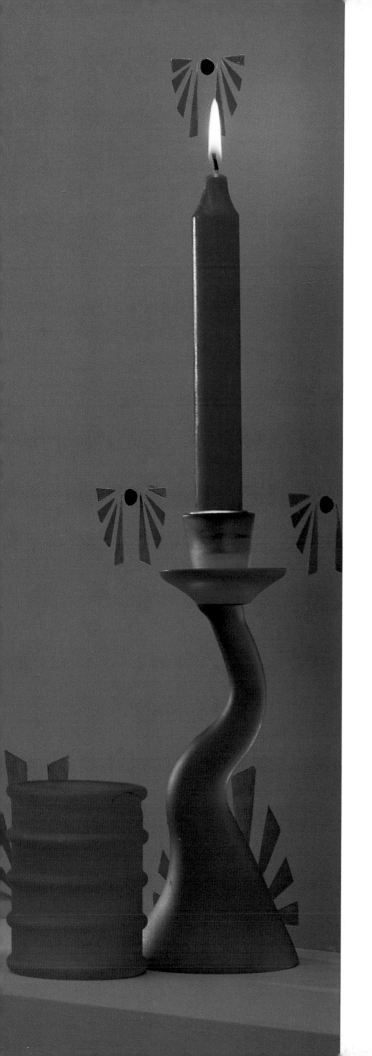

# Chapter 8

# ABSTRACTIONS

*Bold stripes and wild curls, lines and dots, circles, squares and triangles, bubbles and basket weave, cubes and cones: colour your designs in bright singing colours to make a bold statement in your home.*

PREVIOUS PAGE
*A blue plastic vase with clean lines makes an interesting subject for this Art Deco design. The pattern is picked up in different sizes on the wall forming a truly co-ordinating scheme.*

Do you remember when you were at school and the teacher gave you lots of little felt pieces in different shapes and told you to make them into whatever pictures you wanted?

This is what I want you to do now. Make flowers out of circles and triangles or squares and dots. Make skyscrapers out of rectangles and water out of wavy lines. Breaking things down into simple shapes and forms will allow you to create stunning designs in a modern, visually stunning style. This is a wonderful way of creating very personal designs, exploring your creative side to interpret shapes and forms in your own way. You could look at life in that free and uninhibited way when you were a child and you can do it now.

Take a close look at the designs that are featured in this chapter. What could you do with the different elements? For a start you could create some pieces of contemporary art. Take a sheet of water-colour paper and divide it by blocking in

the whole space using five different-sized rectangles in various colours. Then add selected elements into and crossing these rectangles. Instant art. Look at the work of artists like Braque, Klee and Kandinsky for inspiration.

Cut yourself a square of manila card and cut various swirly shapes out of it. Make yourself a lampshade out of the patterned card. When you turn on the light it will cast shadows in the shape of the cut-out pieces. This gives the effect of stencilling with light! Use coloured bulbs for added interest.

Now let's look at a circle. What is it? It can be a sun, a bubble or perhaps a simplified flower. What can we do with it? We can add triangles around the edges of the circle for a more realistic sun. Then we can divide it into two for a setting sun. These two designs combined will make a simple but effective border for a sitting room using gold for the circle and black for the rays. Use the two halves as a border, alternating the

*These unusual mugs and the teapot with their bold stencilled designs make an unusual ornament for a modern room where more traditional designs would be out of place. I used hobby ceramic paints and intend them for decorative purposes only. When I get bored with them I will scrape off the stencilling and replace it with new designs.*

top with the bottom half. To the circle and the triangles add a long, slim line with a few triangles set along it's length. There you have a stem and leaves to complete your flower. Use them vertically in a line, or horizontally, and you have a smart border. Colour the stem and leaves green and the flowers in any colour you like.

Triangles can be long and thin, right-angled or 'facing' in any direction. Make them into stars, trees, grass and leaf segments. Shade them carefully when you colour them in and you will make them look like cones.

Squares and rectangles are next: these can become bricks, window panes and plant pots.

Look at a human figure and what shapes do you see? The head is a circle; the body, a rectangle; four thinner rectangles, arms and legs; four small ovals, hands and feet. You could create a

really effective border of stick figures in your hallway. Make it quite narrow so that the subject matter is not immediately apparent.

Look at some of the more usual stencil designs of flowers, ribbons and leaves. How could you change them to make them into pleasing abstracts?

Fruits can be squared off. The colour of fruit is a great identifier. A square of red blended with green, a triangle of yellowy green and a cluster of purpley squares can easily be identified as apples, pears and grapes, especially if you add a thin triangular stalk to each motif. This would make a really super border for a modern kitchen.

Several wavy blue lines, one atop the other, become water, a few geometric shapes properly assembled become a boat and fish can be constructed from triangles. You can use all these anywhere in your bathroom.

*Green and yellow always look good together, especially so on this little spice rack. The designs in this chapter lend themselves to adaptation, fitting easily around awkward shapes.*

*This piece of gold fabric with its line and bud is destined to be hung on a metal coronet around a bed, or maybe I will make it into cushion covers or perhaps I will drape it over a curtain pole.*

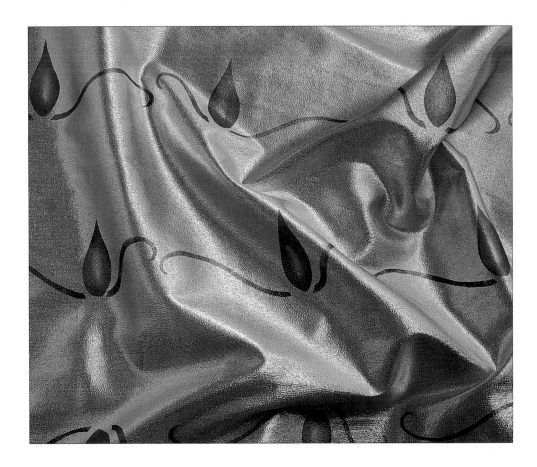

I love swirls in all sizes. Because they are soft and flow nicely they would be very good for a bedroom. Different coloured swirls on top of an inverted triangle become an ice cream and on top of a line they are another flower shape or a tree. Stencil a large design as a border at the height of the dado rail then fill below the border with smaller, randomly placed swirls. Change the rotation of the swirl, as well, for variety.

Now that you have played with the shapes and extended the boundaries of your imagination, just look at the shapes themselves. First, make a row of ten triangles all the same size and shape. In between each one insert an inverted triangle on the same base line. There you have two simple designs. To the first row, after every third triangle, add a taller one. You can go on and on with just this simple three-sided figure to create literally hundreds of designs – the possibilities are endless. This activity will also work with other geometric shapes and it is even more rewarding when you use more than one shape in the same experiment. Rediscover geometry through your stencils.

Personally, I always think that abstract designs look wonderful stencilled in bright, clean colours. Try reds with purple, fuchsia with orange, blues with terracotta and yellow with turquoise. The amount of each colour will affect the look of the stencilling so try a lot of jade green with just a touch of magenta then try it the other way around to see which you prefer.

Although the designs we have looked at would be ideally suited to a modern home with simple stylish decoration there is nothing to stop you using them in a farmhouse or wherever else you want. You could perhaps tone the colours down and use peaches, lemons and pale blues. Making the designs into flower and tree shapes would be ideal as they would look more rustic than modern in that setting.

Art Deco produced a great variety of hard-edged designs. They are all quite beautiful and can be a great inspiration for all designers. A simple Deco design can be stencilled in just one colour or in a multitude of colours or shades. The look of some designs varies greatly depending on which colours you choose, so be sure to practice with a few different colour combinations before embarking on an ambitious project. Art Nouveau designs tended towards more sinuous and swirling patterns.

Books on modern architecture and furniture, art and design and visits to contemporary museums will all be extremely helpful in your quest for inspiration. Look at examples of naive and ethnic painting, as well as African and prehistoric drawings and see what a wealth of shapes you can discover.

These geometric, abstract shapes can sometimes appear more difficult to appreciate than the traditional floral stencil designs. However, abstract shapes and forms can open up a whole world of stencilling opportunties that will stimulate the creative side of your personality and once you have tried them I am sure that you will keep coming back for more.

*Textured stencilling in black, white and purple has been used to great effect on a fuchsia-painted mirror frame. This was a simple project to make using four pieces of wood and a mirrored tile.*

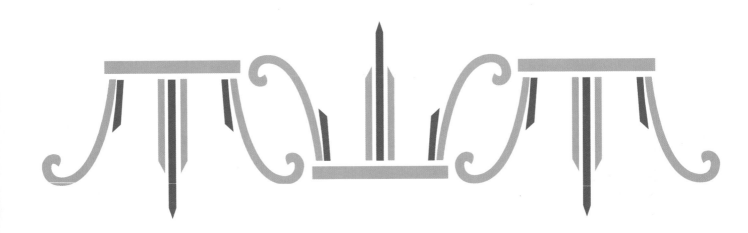

Buds and curving stems make a smart border for curtains, or make them into a circle on your duvet cover.

These triangles have been formed into a light and dark border that is perfect for a sitting room.

This design looks like a crown with its curved outer line. Stencil it in green and orange or green and gold.

The triangle hanging from the arched line can be reversed or stencilled in diagonal lines.

The circle resting on a curvy triangle is ideal for a bathroom and looks good from any angle.

I love sinuous designs and this curling line enclosing the circle would be super in a bedroom.

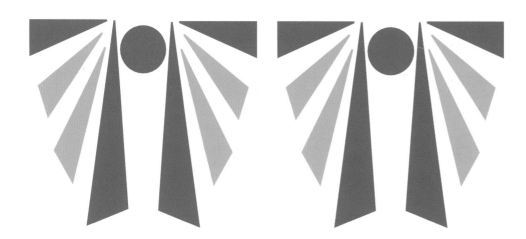

*Use the larger of the two-tier shapes as a border and the smaller as a random motif, either above or below, or use them both together as shown.*

*Small triangles cutting into large circles could be stencilled near the ceiling. Careful shading of the circle, rather than flat painting will be very effective.*

*These lines and circles are reminiscent of flowers. Stencil the lines in green and the circles in blues and lilacs in a random pattern.*

*These tomato-like swirls would look great in shades of red on kitchen tiles.*

*Trace a simple deco design and use coloured pencils to choose your scheme.*

*Stencilled swirls and circles can be rotated to form a random pattern. Magenta and orange is a really vibrant combination.*

Three-cornered squares could
edge your blinds or be spray
etched onto glass.
Circles and curved horns
look best as a small design.
and would look good in
the kitchen.

Thin lines, thick lines
and triangles combine to
form a sophisticated stencil.

Squares and stars can be
used as a stencil on their
own but they are given
movement by the lines. Make
a second overlay for the star.

Stencil these elegant swirls
around your mantelpiece.

Delicate curved lines are
perfect for a bedroom.

Long, sophisticated designs
look wonderful on table legs
or used as a moulding to
imitate wood panels.

# Chapter 9

# DOWN THE GARDEN PATH

*Dovecotes and herb pots, beehives and
orchards, long rows of vegetables and
patterned brick paths, wrought iron gates
and rose-covered arbours, splashing
fountains and lily-filled ponds and a cat
sleeping in the sun: one or more of these
will be essential ingredients in
your dream garden.*

*PREVIOUS PAGE*
*A large picture makes a*
*bold statement in this bright*
*sitting room. Use different*
*floral designs to frame a*
*stencil of your own home. If*
*you get bored with the*
*picture, paint over it and*
*stencil a new masterpiece.*

*ABOVE*
*The hydrangea border has*
*been stencilled over a*
*fireplace putting the*
*finishing touch to a blue*
*and yellow room. The dried*
*flowers were the inspiration*
*for the design.*

Have you ever grown your own vegetables? The excitement in waiting to see the first shoots peep out of the ground is unbearable. Then when you see healthy rows of carrots, peas and brassicas all waiting to be eaten you know the waiting was worthwhile.

You can stencil terracotta markers with images of the vegetables you are growing and stand them at the ends of the rows. However, it is less expensive to stencil a terracotta tile instead and you will have the advantage of a bigger surface area to decorate. If young children visit your garden, stencil similar tiles with wildlife designs and dot them around the garden for the children to find. Use such things as frogs, bees, hedgehogs and wildflowers. It will

keep them busy, especially if you move the tiles around between visits, and may spark off an interest in gardening.

Make your own stencilled seed packets for giving seeds to your friends; you may well find that they become collectors' items. You could also keep a gardener's diary and stencil it with pretty images of your successes.

Why not stencil a garden trug? You can colour-wash it first to match your room then stencil it with delphinium flowers or shell-pink roses. Make a picture for your wall with a mixture of pressed and stencilled flowers and leaves. You can make a themed set of pictures, maybe of bulbs or climbers. You can involve your children here, especially those who are lucky enough to have their own patch of garden, to make a picture of the plants they have grown.

Deck-chair covers, garden parasols, seat cushions and trays are all wonderful subjects for stencilling. Flowers are the first subject that springs to mind but if you live at the seaside you can use shells, waves and fishes. Edge your flower borders with shells too on terracotta edging tiles. Stencil your hammock with one bright bold flower in the style of Georgia O'Keefe and use smaller versions on your sun hat and shawl.

Garden pots can be made regal with acanthus leaves or given a touch of humour with fairies and pets. Even your wheelbarrow can be stencilled but, if you make it look too nice, you may not want to use it for its original purpose. Still, you can always stand plant pots in it and make it into a feature.

Do you have a plain area of wall in your garden, either on the side of your house or on the garden wall itself? Paint the wall a soft blue, make a large design

of a dovecote and stencil it on the wall. When you add the doves in cool greys and white they will swoop around the wall as if in the sky. Large stencils may sound too daunting to attempt. They are not, you know! Just make a smaller design then photocopy it up to the required size. Then, all you have to do is add detail so that the finished item does not look too naive. If you are making a design that has to match on both sides just get one side right then trace it off and reverse it. Easy! I make all my designs onto tracing paper first then, if I want to reverse the design for whatever reason, I just turn the paper over for a mirror image.

A fountain could be stencilled onto that wall, too, or you could stencil one inside your house. The bathroom would be the obvious choice but why not the bedroom or sitting room? There are lots of examples around in garden centres and historic houses from which you can take inspiration. Look at the stencil

*The place mats are made of MDF, painted in spring-green and spattered with dark blue along the edges. Final edging was done with bronze and blue. A selection of vegetables and plants were then stencilled into the centres. You could use flowers, herbs or any other subject dear to your heart.*

*RIGHT*

*This bedroom was lightly colour-washed in a creamy colour and decorated with a mass of flowers. The stencilling is not overpowering as blue and green are peaceful colours. Blossoms tumble towards the headboard but are used more sparingly along the wall at ceiling level. The same colours, when stencilled onto the pale blue background of the bed linen, appear more muted.*

*BELOW*

*In daylight hours the lights look like wall-mounted flower containers, and the stencilling takes on an added dimension, in the evenings, in the light from the glass shades.*

design for Aquarius in this book for an idea of how to stencil water quite simply. If that is not right for you, look at books on art to see how different artists have handled the problem over the years. You are bound to find a style that meets your needs.

Stencilled floors always look wonderful. Make a vibrant flower border on your floor using stencilled flower heads with just a few leaves. You can make it as wide as you like and give it curvy edges for more interest. Look at books by Gertrude Jekyll for instant inspiration. Each person in the household could chose a section of the 'garden' as their own and make a selection of their favourite flowers for the design.

This idea would work just as well on a quilt and could be worked on by a group of people either together or in their own homes.

Make a border for your sitting room of violets, pinks, asters and larkspur. Either make them intertwine or stand each one upright and separate from the rest. Try this with different flowers until you find a combination that you like.

You can, of course, stencil a garden path in your home. Brickwork patterns are really beautiful. Make a herringbone pattern to edge your hallway floor with a circular pattern for the vestibule. Small groups of leaves, such as camomile, stencilled at intervals in the pattern will soften the design and make it more realistic.

A short section of picket fence stencilled onto the wall makes a charming and inexpensive bed head. Vary the height of the posts to create a curve and decorate with stencilled climbing sweet peas or roses.

For a different look, in different bedrooms, group floral designs according to colour. For example, a yellow room would be spectacular with daffodils, roses and lilies. A blue room could have cornflowers, delphiniums and clematis, while a smaller blue room would be pretty with bluebells, speedwell and forget-me-nots. Hydrangeas would look very pretty in a bedroom with pink blooms and pale yellow daisies. Stencil the groups around a bed head and add them to a muslin curtain and your pillowcases and cushions.

A little border of wheelbarrows, garden tools and a watering can is a nice idea for a really keen gardener. You could stencil a real metal watering can with a spray of roses or tulips and use it as a vase indoors. A garden shed could be disguised with a clematis scrambling up its walls.

Pictures of flowers, herbs and gardens abound so you should have little difficulty in finding reference material. The only problem is that you will be spoiled for choice.

Stencil the onion on plain tiles where the transparency of the ceramic paint shows off the delicate skin.

Purple aubergines on a white background make a stunning border in a kitchen.

Roses and violets are ideal flowers to adorn a jewellery box or the back of your hair brush and mirror.

Stencil the cress border around the edges of place mats or on a passe-partout.

Chillies can be red, yellow or orange on your kitchen drawers.

The daisy is a very popular motif. Paint plant pots deep blue and stencil these two motifs with white petals and green leaves.

Try the carrot and cabbage border along the wall just above the tiles.

Irises, named for the rainbow goddess, abound in a huge variety of colours. Stencil them in your bathroom around the top of the bath and as motifs on bath panels.

The hydrangea border would look very pretty in a bedroom.

Violets and leaves stencilled on ribbons as tie backs for curtains is an excellent idea and is a simple project for a beginner.

Dill is another delicate subject for any room in the house. The tiny florets can be any colour, you do not have to be realistic.

The convolvulus design looks complex but it is really made up of lots of small motifs. Use it as it is as a border or take the separate units to make your own version of the design.

The small motif of daisies and forget-me-nots is ideal to border the top of a dressing table with single motifs above drawer handles.

114

Sunflowers look great on door panels and will enliven curtains and blinds. Make a separate overlay for the flower centres and leaves.

The tulip motif is quite abstract and can be used in a study or workroom.

The urn can be made larger for a skirting-level border or as a showpiece. You could fill it with your favourite plants and flowers.

Use the leaf around windows or reverse-stencil it onto the back of a chair.

Trees in the style of Clarice Cliffe are ideal for a deco style dining room.

Use the nasturtium on napkins or as a bright border.

# Chapter 10

# FAR AND WIDE

*Greek temples and desert islands,
Italian ice-creams and pasta shapes,
castanets and the tiled Alhambra
Gardens, Scottish tartan designs and
Aztec patterns: the world is your oyster.
Pick your favourite location and make
yourself a theme room where you can
dream of far away places.*

*PREVIOUS PAGE*
*I stripped these drawers down to the bare wood and decided to make a little bulb and seed storage unit. The brightly coloured drawer fronts are colour coded to make selection easy. The Dutch tulip stencil was the most appropriate finishing touch.*

*ABOVE*
*A simple cane shelving unit was painted red and black and decorated with the Mount Fujiyama stencil to create a serene atmosphere for an oriental bedroom.*

Do you have any rooms with small windows that do not give much light? Design a window frame and stencil it onto the wall. Then you can give yourself a view. Let your imagination take flight. If you want to live in the Italian countryside stencil cypress trees with rows of soft green vines (simplified, of course) leading to a terracotta-tile-roofed villa. Don't forget the golden sunshine.

Stencil an English landscape with stone walls, oak trees and blossom in the hedgerows. A thatched cottage with its traditional cottage garden would be fun whilst a formal lawn with fountains, statuary and peacocks would be much more sophisticated.

Try an old fashioned seascape with clippers, their sails fully furled or a

peaceful Cornish harbour with brightly coloured boats reflected in the water and seagulls soaring overhead. There is no end to the vistas you can create. Take your time to decide what you want in the view. Design all the pieces separately if you want, then fit them all together using tracing paper.

Scottish and Irish tartans can be stencilled onto cushions or perhaps in the space between the dado-rail and the skirting board. There are lots to choose from in wonderful colours and intricate patterns. You may even become interested in the history of the patterns and the stories behind the weaves.

Take a few minutes to write down what first comes into your mind when you think of Spain. It may be dancers, matadors, castanets or even cane-wrapped wine bottles. For me it is Barcelona with its Art Nouveau architecture. It does not matter what you choose to decorate your theme room, it will be equally evocative simply because the subject matter is your own choice. A theme room does not have to be over the top. The right choice of colours is often all it takes, along with perhaps a few well chosen souvenirs.

Blue, yellow and terracotta will give your room a Provençal look whilst cream, white and blues will take you further north to Scandinavia.

Look at the picture of the Japanese shelves in this section. Why not stencil your bedroom wall with the black and white screen design? Place a small straight table against the wall and stencil a simple floral arrangement in the ikebana style on the wall to make it look

*This very simple design of a Shinto temple gateway is ideal for these delicate oil burners.*

*This tray decorated with urns and columns is ideal for serving drinks and snacks on a hot summer's day. The background was created by swirling an artist's brush over a layer of green glaze. Tablecloths and deck chairs could be stencilled with the same motif to unify your patio.*

as though it is standing on the table. (Stencil the table as well if you can't find one to suit.) Make a stencil of Japanese maple leaves, and stencil them in grey on the wall to look like shadows. Slight touches of colour could show through where the leaves are 'touching' but not too much. Try to get the effect using real foliage and tracing paper and you will see what I mean.

Stencil your kitchen with a selection of food from your chosen country. This could be as simple as a border of pasta shapes. Add glass storage jars filled with the real thing, jars of olive oil and old wine bottles dripping with candle wax for maximum effect.

You don't have to stencil a whole rainforest to create a tropical mood. Leafy borders, motifs and a large stencilled monstera plant will do the trick. Add a bird of paradise and a trailing hibiscus for colour then turn up the thermostat.

Perhaps you want to cool down? Stencil a waterfall from ceiling to floor. Add stencils of cool but exotic waterside plants and shiny wet rocks for the water to splash onto, and you have created an idyllic spot on a desert island.

Stencil each drawer of a chest of drawers, the top and both sides of the piece with flowers from a different country. Carry this theme onto the wardrobe panels and the bed head to create a really wonderful suite of furniture that could be a treasured heirloom for years to come.

How about stencilling a study with a selection of masks and head dresses? There are wonderful African masks in blacks, browns and reds, often with animals built into the design. There are Venetian masks either in plain white or full of exuberant detail. Create a collage effect by adding real lace or sequins. Look to Mardi Gras costumes or the native American Indians for head dresses.

If you want something from really far and away try stencilling a world of your own. This can be a fantasy land of turreted castles and the misty 'faerie'

realm. The subject may sound childish but you can make highly sophisticated designs. This is an area of great interest at the moment and you could stencil your own designs taken from a favourite scene in a fantasy novel.

We are bombarded with images from all around the world every day of our lives so there is no shortage of reference material. Travel brochures and guides; books on costume, food and lifestyles will all be helpful. If you have already travelled to your ideal locations all the better, but, with a few touches of enthusiastic stencilling, you can bring the world to your doorstep.

*This is a spectacular South African flower and is a wonderful subject for stencilling. I stencilled a large motif to create a focal point in an uncluttered sitting room.*

Shamrocks look wonderful on vases, napkins and tablecloths.

The cowboy boot would look great in a children's room. Make a separate overlay for the decoration.

Colour venetian masks in bright colours. Make a separate overlay for the eyes.

Easter Island heads are simple but evocative. Cut one overlay for the outer shape and one for the eyes and chin shadow.

You can extend the column by moving the base line. Make the base by inverting the top two elements. Cut a separate stencil for the dark areas.

The boomerang can spin around your room as a motif or a border. Try using colour glazes for a change. Use one overlay for the shape and one for the stripes.

Bread and wine glasses will enliven your kitchen. Don't forget to change the angle of the liquid in the glasses if you tilt them. Use one overlay for the bread and wine glass shapes, and another for the decoration on the bread, the wine and the highlight on the glass.

124

The Taj Mahal would look marvellous stencilled in white, cream and pale grey on a blue background or on a ground of sunset colours. Make a separate overlay for the dark areas.

The Mount Fujiyama design is quite a simple stencil. You can use all the elements separately or together. Cut two overlays for the mountain.

The Shinto temple gate is just great for a minimalist lifestyle.

Spanish dancers wear the most brilliant dresses. Use the design on muslin curtains or on vases.

The protea is a beautiful South African flower. It is a wonderful shade of pink with grey overtones. Stencil it as a stunning border or as a motif on silk cushions.

Tulips can be stencilled in bright colours or perhaps just pink on white on tiles. You could even have a black tulip with green or gold leaves.

The London bus can trundle around your kitchen in its traditional red.

The windmill would look perfect stencilled blue on a white bulb bowl.

Stencil this simple urn in rows in varying sizes. Colour some in terracotta with a sponged green area to represent moss. You could even even add other designs such as grapes or keys.

Koala bears would look adorable climbing the sides of your child's window. Cut a separate stencil for the dark nose and ears.

Prickly cactus would look best in a dusky green and could be mixed with the cowboy boot for an interesting border.

# MATERIALS
# AND TECHNIQUES

## WHAT IS A STENCIL?

A stencil is any paper cut out with holes or 'windows' through which you can paint colour onto a chosen surface. The stencil can be as simple or intricate as you wish, from a design on a single sheet, or overlay, used with just one colour, to several overlays using many colours.

Each part of the stencil has a role to play. The holes form the pattern and the spaces between, which are called bridges or ties, separate the different elements and give a sense of realism and depth to the design.

## MATERIALS

CARD: The most traditional material for making a stencil is manila card. This is a heavy-gauge card that has been soaked in linseed oil to make it waterproof. Ideally it should be used with oil-based or spray paints, because water-based paints will eventually make it soggy and unusable.

The advantage of using manila card is that it is easy to cut. Its main disadvantage is that you can't see through it, which is important when you line up your design comprising more than one overlay. The answer is to cut registration marks into the edges of the stencil, which can be matched with each overlay. Alternatively you can simply select one or two elements of the design and cut them out of each overlay. But remember to only paint them once.

ACETATE: Draughtsmen's acetate is the best type for stencilling. But always choose the right weight for the job. If it won't bend around corners easily; if it is too thin it will tear. Acetate is shiny on one side and slightly opaque on the other. It is long lasting, easy to clean and you can see through it for easy registration. Draw directly onto the opaque side of the acetate with a pencil and paint onto the shiny side, but remember that the image will be reversed when you turn the acetate over. Wipe your stencil clean from time to time to prevent a build up of paint in the windows.

PAPER: Providing you are not going to put your stencil to extensive use, you can make it from heavy paper or cardboard. Both are easy to draw on, easy to cut and have the added bonus of being inexpensive. However, unless you use heavy tracing paper, you will not be able to see through your stencil for registration purposes.

METAL: Stencils made from thin brass are long-lasting and easy to clean, but you can't see through them for registration and they are difficult to cut.

OTHERS: You can use a piece of lace or paper doilies to create a pretty stencil and interesting, if delicate, effects on walls and furniture. A few coats of varnish will strengthen them long enough for limited use.

*Stencils in a Japanese-style design have transformed this simple cane shelving unit to create a serene atmosphere for an oriental bedroom.*

## EQUIPMENT

*As stencilling requires very little basic equipment, it is worth investing in a good cutting utensil and brushes. The surface to be decorated will dictate the paints to be used.*

BRUSHES: It is easy to recognise the traditional stencil brush by its round stock and flat-cut bristles. It's a specialised design which hasn't changed for centuries. You can buy brushes in a variety of sizes, each one designed for a particular task. The largest brushes, with the biggest stock, are suitable for floors and those stencils with larger windows in their design. The smallest brushes are for the tiniest details. I prefer to use the largest brushes possible, as they seem to blend the colours so much better.

As stencilling continues to increase in popularity, brushes and other tools of the trade are readily available from art supply shops and specialist stencil stores. If you have difficulty in finding stencil brushes you can use an ordinary paint brush, but unfortunately they are not so adept when you're blending colours. It is also possible to use an old shaving brush, but you must cut the bristles flat across the top. Do not use an expensive brush as the bristles will be too soft.

Be sure to clean your brushes throughly when you have finished work. If you look after them they will last a lifetime.

SPONGES: Try experimenting with a sea sponge to apply the colour. This will give a beautifully dappled effect to your stencilling. And a mixture of brushed and sponged stencilling on one project will add texture to your chosen design.

PAINTS: If stencillers of bygone days could see the selection of paints and the range of colours available today they would be positively green with envy!

You should have no trouble at all in finding the right paint in the right colour for whatever project you have in mind. You can use many types of paint for stencilling, depending on the effect you wish to achieve. All you have to do is match the paint to the surface, whether plaster, wood, fabric or glass, and use common sense. For example you should always use non-toxic paints in children's rooms.

ACRYLICS: These are available from all good art supply shops and come in a wonderful array of colours, including pearl and metallic finishes. They are fast drying and can blend easily. As acrylic paints are water based you can thin them with water, and you can clean your brushes quite easily afterwards with warm soapy water. The fast drying qualities of acrylics make them ideal for stencilling.

STENCIL PAINTS: These are also water-based, but are normally sold in pots and are more liquid in form than most artist's acrylics. As they are specially made for stencilling, they are very fast drying so you can get on with your project much quicker. Brushes may be cleaned in warm water.

OIL PAINTSTICKS: As the name suggests, this is oil paint, but it is specially formulated into sticks that look like chunky wax crayons. They are very easy to use and the colours blend beautifully. As the crayons are 'self healing' they do not dry out and will last for simply ages. The only drawback is that, as the paint is oil-based, you will have to clean your brushes with white spirit before washing them in soapy water.

CREAMS: Stencil paints in cream form are a new addition to the range of paints available to the stenciller. They are a solid paint in a jar so you can hold them in your hand while stencilling and just dip in your brush when it needs reloading. Cream paints are suitable for use on all surfaces including fabric.

SPRAY PAINTS: Many professional decorators use car or other spray paints for stencilling. They are available in a large range of colours including metallic. No brushes are required as you just spray the paint directly on to your chosen surface. More often than not you can use just one overlay, as the wonderful effects are obtained by subtle use of the spray. The great disadvantage of spray paints is that they can be very messy, so you must protect surrounding areas with newspaper to stop the paint spreading. They are also quite difficult to use until you get the pressure on the nozzle just right. Do not be discouraged by all this as the final results can be quite stunning.

FABRIC PAINTS: There are many different makes of fabric paint available which can be used in the same way as acrylics and other water-based paints. Many can be fixed by ironing or by tumble drying. You can stencil onto most fabrics but natural ones such as cotton, linen and silk are the best.

CERAMIC PAINTS: These paints are for use on tiles, pottery vases, tableware and other ceramic items. Unless you have access to a kiln, only use those paints that don't need firing. Bear in mind that these paints are for purely decorative purposes and, as such, will not stand up to a lot of washing or the dishwasher. So don't think about decorating the dinner service just yet!

JAPAN PAINTS: These are oil-based paints which are also extremely fast drying, making them perfect for stencilling. The range of colours, however, is not extensive.

OTHERS: You can use any kind of paint for stencilling as long as you match the paint to the surface. Beautiful effects can be achieved with watercolour paint; however, this should be thickened by mixing with a little acrylic paint. I often use it un-thickened on heavy watercolour paper and let the colour bleed. Not very traditional, but different!

All water-based household paints can be used but they often take too long to dry, which can be a disadvantage if you are trying to decorate your room with a multicoloured border or frieze.

Wood stains and varnishes also give interesting effects. You can obviously use them on wood, but clear varnish mixed with a little oil paint can be quite beautiful as a decoration on glassware.

Always follow the manufacturers' instructions. Some paints, as well as solvents, can be dangerous!

*As you become more confident you will be able to stencil large images, floors and ceramics with ease. Although the designs in this room are all quite different, their colours are reflected in the patchwork tablecloth.*

## PREPARATION OF SURFACES

As with all forms of decorating, the surface must be prepared to accept the paint you have chosen. If you don't do the groundwork, you will not get good results. Dust and grit under the stencil will prevent it from lying flat and make the paint bleed under the stencil paper.

WALLS: Remove all traces of old wallpaper and fill in any holes. It's not necessary for walls to be perfectly smooth; it all depends on the look you want to achieve. Allow newly decorated walls to dry out thoroughly before stencilling. You can stencil onto bare plaster, but treat it first with clear universal sealant.

PAINTED SURFACES: You can paint onto virtually any painted surface providing it is properly prepared. Gloss paint must be 'keyed' by sanding first. You should not have to seal your stencil with varnish unless it is to receive heavy use. Varnish the whole surface, not just the stencilled area as varnish tends to yellow slightly with age.

WOOD: Remove any wax or varnish and strip off old paint using a proprietary stripper following manufacturers' instructions. If the surface is very rough, sand it first with a coarse sandpaper, followed by a 'wet and dry' sandpaper to give it a final smooth finish. Don't forget to always paint with the grain.

GLASS: The only prerequisite here is that the glass should be clean, dry and free of grease.

FABRIC: Fabric should always be pre-washed to remove any trace of dressing and then ironed. The dressing can cause the paint to bleed and ruin your stencilling.

WOODEN FLOORS: Using coarse sandpaper then grading down to a 'wet and dry' sandpaper, sand the floor, with the grain, to give a 'key'. When you've finished, vacuum and wipe down with a lint-free cloth. For an old floor, you may have to use an industrial sander to get a smooth surface and to get rid of any old varnish and polish. Sand the corners and edges by hand. When you have finished stencilling, seal the floor with at least two coats of colourless varnish and your work of art will last for years.

METAL: Remove old paint using the correct proprietary stripper. Remove any rust with a wire brush and sand the metal with steel wool. Stencil directly onto the metal or paint first with a metal primer. Oil based paints are best to use on metal as they help prevent rust; remember to seal your stencilling with a coat of clear varnish.

CERAMICS: Ensure the surface is clean, dry and free from grease, then stencil directly onto the surface using ceramic paints. Again seal with a proprietary varnish to give your work a longer life.

PLASTIC: Before stencilling always 'key' the surface with fine sandpaper. You can also paint the plastic first, then stencil onto the paint.

PAPER: You can stencil onto most types of paper, although a textured wallpaper is not an ideal surface as it will break up your design.

## LINING UP

The following instructions for lining up your stencils are guide lines only. You can position a border with great scientific precision, only to find that it looks rather odd in a room that is not perfectly square.

CENTRE POINTS: All you need are two pieces of string. Pin the end of one piece of string in one corner and pin the other end in the opposite corner. Repeat the procedure with the second piece of string in the two remaining corners. The place where the strings cross is your centre point.

VERTICALS AND HORIZONTALS: To find the true vertical of a wall you will need a plumb line. Coat the string with chalk and attach the plumb line, fairly high up, on the wall. Let the plumb line settle. Then, holding the plumb weight steadily against the wall with one hand, 'twang' the string. This will leave a line of chalk on the wall.

A spirit-level and a ruler or a tape measure are all you need to find a horizontal line. Decide at what height from the floor you want your stencil. Measure this height at intervals along the wall with chalk or a soft pencil. Then attach a piece of string to the wall at both sides so it runs along the marks and draw in the horizontal line.

BORDERS AND FRIEZES: Always begin in the middle and work outwards. You may find that the design will fit the space available using the exact number of repeats. If the design almost fits the space, you can stretch it or compress it slightly as you work, but if there is just too much space left over, you can take some of the elements from the stencil and make a corner motif.

ROUNDING CORNERS: You may find it easier to treat each wall individually and use a corner motif on each one. This method works rather nicely around a door frame, putting the corner motif at the base of the frame and again at the top corners.

An acetate stencil will bend into a corner and you will be able to carry on stencilling without interruption. Don't forget that if you are stencilling a border around a whole room, your design will have to join together at some point, so be prepared!

MITRING CORNERS: Draw a pencil line at 45 degrees into the corner. Then put a strip of masking tape against your pencil line and stencil up to the tape. Move the masking tape to the other side of the pencilled line and match the stencilling into the corner. As this can be tricky, always do a dummy run on a piece of paper before attempting the real thing.

MOTIFS: You can place motifs on the wall or floor in a random manner using your eye as a guide. You can, if you wish be more precise and draw up a grid. To do this, simply attach one end of a piece of string to the centre of one wall, at floor level, and the other end to the centre of the opposite wall. Mark the position of the string on the floor, move the string an equal distance along the two walls and make the next set of marks. Continue until you have all the lines you need and then repeat using the two remaining walls. Now you can place the motifs as desired.

## STENCILLING TECHNIQUES

To fix your stencil to the wall you can use low-tack masking tape positioned along the outside edges of the stencil. This will keep it secure, but won't remove your paint surface. Alternatively, you can spray the back of the stencil with spray adhesive. This also holds the stencil in place, but allows you to peel it away from the surface and reposition more easily. Always use in a well ventilated room.

APPLYING THE PAINT: The best advice I can give you is to practise your stencil on a piece of paper first. The other golden rules are always to use a dry, clean brush, and never to overload it with colour as this will cause the paint to seep under the edges of the stencil paper and smudge the design. A dirty brush will taint your colours.

USING PAINT STICKS: These have a 'sealing skin' over the surface to prevent the paint from drying out. To obtain the colour and break the seal, simply rub the point of the stick onto a separate piece of acetate. Pick up the colour on your brush by rubbing it gently into the paint, using first a clockwise and then an anticlockwise movement. Hold your brush at right angles to the stencil and apply the paint using the same circular strokes. Always start by applying the paint around the edges of the cut-out areas first. This will create a lighter area in the middle, as the colour is worked off, and is the first step in shading your design.

USING STENCIL PAINTS: Don't use the paint straight from the pot or tube because you will invariably overload your brush. Put a little of the paint onto a saucer and, if necessary, thin down with the appropriate thinning agent to get better consistency.

Dip the brush into the paint, wetting only the ends of the bristles. Now take most of it off again on a paper towel or newspaper by rubbing the bristles gently clockwise and then anticlockwise onto the paper. When your brush is practically dry, apply the paint gently to the stencil, again using the circular movements. Begin painting at the edges of the cut-out areas, working to the centre to give a shaded effect.

USING FABRIC PAINTS: Make sure that your fabric is laid out flat, with a layer of absorbent paper underneath as some lightweight fabrics will allow paint to seep through. This is the one occasion when you can use a damp brush because the fabric will absorb a lot of moisture.

The procedure now is exactly the same as for water-based paints. However, I recommend using spray adhesive to hold the stencil in place as you will not be able to remove any paint that seeps under the edges.

USING CERAMIC PAINTS: When applying this paint it is better to use a stippling motion. Hold the brush at right angles to the stencil and, by flexing your wrist, make a gentle dabbing motion with the brush onto the cut-out areas.

USING SPRAY PAINTS: Practise with the spray paints before you commit yourself to your project, as it takes some time to produce the gentle 'whoosh' that indicates the pressure on the nozzle is just right.

Hold a piece of cardboard, as a guard, at an angle against the part of the stencil you are trying to paint and spray towards that. The paint will just drift onto the stencil and the windows will not become clogged. You need just the lightest film of paint with each coat.

If you use a stencil with a single overlay you may get some overspill from one colour to the next, but sometimes this creates beautiful effects.

SHADING: While it is perfectly acceptable to stencil with simple colours, say green for the leaves and blue for the flowers, you will get a much more professional effect if you add shading to the design, giving it realism.

Shading can be added merely by putting colour on the outer edges of the pattern, leaving a paler area in the centre, rather like a patch of sunlight. You can also get a similar effect by painting lightly all over the design in one colour, then adding another, stronger coat around the edges. Several different colours may also be used for shading. For example, when shading a blue flower, I'll also add a hint of purple to the shadow area. Where a leaf curls behind a flower, the flower colour can be used to shade the leaf. After all, this happens naturally! So, if you stencil a complex pattern, don't worry if some of the colour spills over into other parts of the design.

CUTTING YOUR STENCILS: Use a new blade in your knife or scalpel for each stencil and change it regularly. A blunt blade will rip your stencil rather than cut it cleanly. Put your stencil material on the cutting base and place one hand on the acetate or manila card to keep it steady. Take the craft knife or scalpel and make firm, smooth cuts, always toward yourself but away from the hand steadying the stencil. Cut each window in one stroke for the cleanest edge. Always begin at the centre of the design and work outward, cutting the smallest windows first. If you cut the largest ones first, the stencil will lose strength and subsequent cuts may tear the bridges. Leave a border of about 2ins (5cm) around the cut-out pattern to stop paint spilling over the edges.

MENDING DAMAGED STENCILS: Just put a strip of masking tape over both sides of the rip and simply recut that area.

*When starting a new stencil, take the first colour and apply the paint lightly to the surface, in this case the leaf area of the design.*

*With a clean brush apply the second colour, using the same technique.*

*Create interesting shading by applying a third colour to give depth and realism to certain areas of the design, for instance, under the leaf or on the outer edges of petals.*

*Finally, apply the fourth colour, again using a clean brush.*

## STEP-BY-STEP INSTRUCTIONS

Trace your chosen design either from our trace patterns or from a reference book onto good-quality tracing paper, using a soft pencil. If you are cutting your stencil in acetate, trace the design directly onto the non-shiny side of the acetate. Remember the image will be reversed when you stencil as you always paint over the shiny side of the acetate. To avoid image reversal, place the design under glass and the acetate on top of the glass. Cut the acetate following the lines visible through the glass.

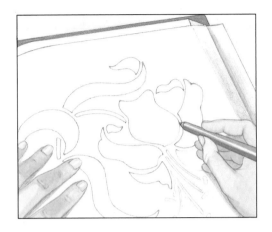

If the design is not the right size for your purposes, you may need to reduce or increase its size. To do this take a sheet of tracing paper drawn with a squared grid, then trace the design. Take another sheet of grid paper with either smaller or larger squares, as required, and copy the design square by square onto the new grid.

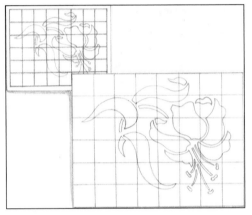

If you are making your stencil from manila card, you will need to transfer the traced design onto the card. Do this by rubbing the reverse of the tracing paper with a very soft pencil. Then place the tracing paper, right side up, onto the card and rework the outline using a hard pencil to transfer the image onto the card.

To cut a manila card or acetate stencil simply lay the acetate or card on a sheet of glass (with the edges bound in masking tape to prevent accidents) or on a self-healing cutting board. Using a new blade and scalpel or craft knife, cut out the stencil using firm, smooth cuts. Always cut toward yourself but away from the hand holding the stencil. Cut each window in one stroke for the cleanest edge.

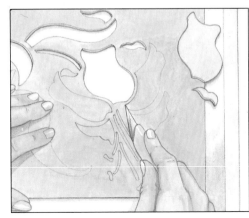

Position the stencil onto the surface you are decorating. Secure with either low-tack masking tape or spray adhesive. The latter helps you reposition the stencil several times without damaging the surface, so is probably more helpful for beginners. Always use in a well ventilated room.

Apply a little paint to a dry brush. Work most of the paint off the brush on to a dry paper towel or newspaper. It is much better to apply the paint in several thin layers rather than in a single thick one which will only cause the paint to seep under the stencil paper and smudge your work.

Holding the brush like a pencil in one hand and supporting the stencil with the other, apply the paint to the cut-out areas of the stencil using light circular movements, in both clockwise and anticlockwise directions. Build up the colour and shading gradually.

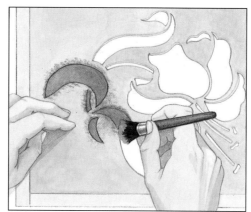

When you have completed the stencil, gently remove it from the surface. Using the registration points, reposition on the surface and continuing stencilling until you have completed the required length. For simple designs you can reposition the design by eye only. Clean away any build up of paint on the stencil as necessary.

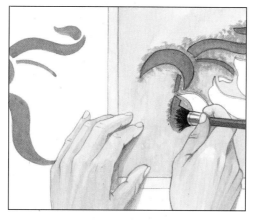

If you have more overlays for additional colours, position each one in succession over the stencilled area. Again use the registration points. You should not have to wait long before using additional overlays as most stencil paints dry rapidly. Always remember to use a clean brush for each new colour.

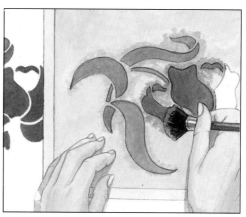

## CREATING DESIGNS

These are examples of what you can achieve with just one simple motif. I made the single tulip motif and decided to see how many other designs I could create with it. As you can see, there are nine more designs shown here and it was only lack of space that made me stop. See if you can find any more.

Enlarge some of the motifs and mix them back in with the smaller ones. This will change the look of the design enormously. You could also square off the motif by taking away the curves and replacing them with straight lines.

Now trace some of the designs and try colouring them in with coloured pencils. Make a monochrome border; then try green leaves with yellow, red or pink petals. Next, try a set of motifs with flowers in mixed colours. Try to use unusual colours such as gold leaves and black petals. Playing around with designs in this way will teach you a lot about the art of stencilling, and will enable you to develop both your design and your colour sense.

# INDEX

The page numbers in *italics* refer to
the illustrations.

## ACKNOWLEDGEMENTS

We would like to thank the following people who have allowed us to stencil and photograph in their homes: Declan and Gail McGoff, Roy and Janet Wood, Katy Wood, Leo and Sophie, Tony and Maureen McIntyre, and John and Karen Meehan (in another home).

I would also like to thank my friends Anne Heywood for her sewing and Ginny Littlewood for laughing with me during adversity.
My husband has contributed vastly to the production of this book, not only with his superb photography but with his creativity and the making of many of the project items.

## GLOSSARY

*US readers may not be familiar with some of the terms used in the book.*

| UK | US |
|---|---|
| bath | bathtub |
| blind | window shade |
| card (stencil) | cardboard |
| dado rail | chair rail |
| muslin | butter muslin |
| skirting board | baseboard |

Many people have lent us props for the photography and we would therefore like to thank:-

Daisy & Tom Ltd (for toys)
81 Kings Road
London SW3 4NX

Raysun Group Ltd.
(for ornaments)
Randall House
Thorbgurgh Road
Scarborough
N. Yorks.
YO11 3UX

Harriet and Dee
7 Police Street
Manchester

Isis (for crystal balls, magic wands etc.)
The Coliseum
Church Street
Manchester

Horus (for Egyptian goods)
The Coliseum
Church Street
Manchester
M4 1PN

Blue Yonder (for sword, gauntlet and armoury)
The Coliseum
Church Street
Manchester
M4 1PN

Nigel Hubbell (for the metal tree)
available from
Creative Originals
The Coliseum
Manchester
M4 1PN

Windhorse Trading
(for candles, chimes, mobiles etc)
3 Coral Park
Henley Road
Cambridge
CB1 3EA

Wax Lyrical (for candle sticks)
12 St Anne's Square
Manchester
M2 7HW

Spoils Kitchen Reject Shops PLC (for towels, vases etc.)
The Arndale Centre
Manchester

Peter Christian Antiques
400/402 Waterloo Road
Blackpool
FY4 4BL

## LIST OF SUPPLIERS

UK
Elrose Products Ltd
20/21 Heronsgat Road
Chorleywood
Hertfordshire WD3 5BN

The Stencil Library
Nesbitt Hill Head
Stamfordham
Northumberland

Michelle Huberman
Fashion n Foil Magic
PO Box 3746
LONDON
N2 9DE

Paddy Vickery Designs
1 West End Grove
Farnham
Surrey GU9 7EG

Relief Stencilling
The Walled Garden
Dolforgan Hall
Kerry
Newtown
Powys SY16 4DN

AUSTRALIA
Stencil House Property Ltd
PO Box 141
Olinda
Victoria 3788

USA
Dressler Stencil Company
253 SW 41st Street
Department V
Renton
WA 98055

Yowler and Shepps
3259 Main Street
Department V
Conestoga
PA 17516

Stencil Artisans League Inc (S.A.L.I.),
PO Box 920109
Norcross
Georgia 30092

S.A.L.I. is a friendly non profit-making organisation whose members work to promote stencilling throughout the world. Members are kept up to date with all the latest products and techniques.